Collaborative School Self-Review

Sheila Russell started her career in education as a mathematics teacher where she learned the importance of seeking to give some power and control to those learning in difficult and stressful situations. She worked for several years as a local authority Senior Education Inspector, advising schools on school development planning, financial planning and equal opportunities. In 1993 she took up the post of Visiting Fellow at Leeds Metropolitan University. She has led OFSTED inspections in primary and secondary schools and now has research interests in school improvement and accountability, and the effects of these pressures on the lives of teachers.

Sheila Russell has written a handbook of guidance for schools on action planning after inspection (*Ready for Action*, Courseware Publications, 1995) and a practical guide to OFSTED inspection (*Prepared for Inspection*, Courseware Publications, 1996). She bases her writing on her experiences of involvement with individual teachers working for change in their organisations, gained through lecturing, training, research, consultancy and support.

Collaborative School Self-Review

Sheila Russell

Published in Great Britain 1996 by Lemos & Crane
20 Pond Square
Highgate
London N6 6BA

Telephone 0181 348 8263

ISBN 1-898001-26-X

A CIP catalogue record for this book is available from the British
Library.

Cover design by Richard Newport
Text design and formatting by The Design Works, Reading
Printed by Biddles, Guildford

Contents

List of figures in text

••

School planning sheets

Foreword

· ·

by Harry Tomlinson

Sheila Russell has a thorough understanding of the wider educational environment in which schools function and a sound knowledge of classroom practice. She displays an ability to explore and focus the research evidence sharply on the issues. Her humanistic approach is based on her evident knowledge of the culture of different schools and an understanding of individual teachers' needs. Sheila knows and shows explicitly how schools can become more effective. Here there is a basis for schools to determine their own futures.

The associated complex issues she deals with openly. She has too high an opinion of the capacity of teachers to learn not to deal clearly with these difficulties. There are definitions of planning, monitoring and self-evaluation, and the relationships between them are made clear. The process for collaborative self-review is shown fully. The focus is intensely on school improvement. Difficult but crucial areas such as classroom observation and the monitoring and evaluation of individual performance are explored imaginatively. The opening of the classroom door is primarily for the sharing of practical knowledge.

There is a need for greater rigour in planning, monitoring and evaluation, particularly as schools are not good at evaluation. Sheila Russell has high expectations of teachers as reflective practitioners. They will need to develop new skills, such as peer observation, clinical supervision and coaching. Relationships between teachers, however, may become more difficult as managers have to learn to be assertive in insisting on school improvement. Arguably appraisal has had limited impact because of the failure to confront similar problems.

This book is both soundly based in research and highly pragmatic. There is guidance about how a school can evaluate the independent learning learning of pupils, and the recognition that every school must determine its own unique agenda. A rigorous monitoring of both maintenance and development activities is essential to provide a basis for the evaluation of quality. The new world of accountability, external and internal is quietly accepted. Schools need to have the resourcefulness to work with their parents, community and OFSTED for school improvement.

With the courage to accept the agenda that Sheila Russell recommends, schools can further develop their skills to strengthen improvements in the quality of learning. Sheila has an intense respect for teachers which is why this book asks a great deal of them on behalf of children. She challenges schools to have the creativity and strength of purpose to commit themselves, even when under intense pressure, to use the processes she recommends to learn from collaborative self-review.

I commend this book. It has style and significance.

Harry Tomlinson
National Chairman
British Educational Management
and Administration Society (BEMAS)

Introduction

There is an urgency about school improvement that is recognised at least as much by those who work in schools as by anyone else, but it is vital to be realistic in reacting to this sense of urgency.

> Administrators and academics, working outside the classroom and animated by political and intellectual agendas for change, may hope for a simpler and more sudden process of change. Too often, however, they express their hopes for change in programmes and imperatives that teachers experience as arbitrary or wrong-headed. Collaborative enquiry offers a slower, more generous and more powerful path towards educational change, and impels those outside schools who hope for change to approach teachers with respect. Proposals for change in teachers' practice are proposals to change teachers' lives, and should be approached with care and humility, not arrogance and certainty.
>
> (Louden, 1991)

This book is about collaborating to create a system for improvement that is unique to a school, based on principles that fit its culture, context and values. It is intended to stimulate debate through practical activities at school level. The

planning sheets (see pp. 199 to 212) can support collaboration and co-ordination but do not prescribe styles or
methods.

School self-review and evaluation, target setting, monitoring and
performance indicators are phrases that have achieved a new
currency in education. They are often associated, relatively
uncritically, with the aim of raising standards and improving schools. In this book monitoring and evaluation are
explored as concepts that need to be questioned, and made
real and practically useful. Chapters deal with questions
about school self-review such as:

- what is it?
- why do it?
- how can it be done?
- how often?
- by whom?
- what difference does it make?

Chapter 1 discusses the dilemmas of accountability and
autonomy that are the background to the pressure for
schools to use self-review as a means of maintaining and
improving standards. Chapters 2 to 5 introduce key practical principles of planning, target setting, monitoring and
evaluation. The theme of choosing methods that fit the

school and the people who work there, while taking account of national pressures, requirements and concern for standards, is woven through the practical advice and guidance. The notion of local, contextually appropriate, solutions to adopting an effective system of self-review is brought to the fore in Chapter 6, which deals with establishing a climate for reflecting on teaching and learning. Accounts of school strategies are used to illuminate the need to take account of people's emotions, relationships and personal expectations. Chapter 7 examines internal and external partnerships that can provide the driving and sustaining force for continuing improvement.

Readers may wish to select from the chapters, and a *summary* at the start of each chapter gives guidance about the contents. Sections introduced by the words 'for consideration' are designed to afford an opportunity for individual or group reflection on the present culture and conditions in any school. School planning sheets are illustrated by hypothetical examples of partially completed sheets, and can be adapted for use in any school as appropriate.

It is hoped that those using the book will be enabled to create their own means of improvement with an energy and commitment based on each individual's personal sense of accountability. The discussion and presentation of ideas can support a school that creates a self-review system in its own way, intending to conserve energies, to broadcast success and to keep the school on its chosen developmental track.

1 Freedom and accountability

∙∙

This chapter presents the policy issues that are the background to the introduction of systems of school self-review. With delegated finance and increasing autonomy schools face changing expectations, from within the school community and from outside. This chapter deals with some of the dilemmas of meeting those changed expectations. Standards and quality are monitored and reported on nationally, and schools are expected to seek new means of raising standards and improving their work. There is an emphasis on external measures of accountability, for instance through performance tables and inspection, which can appear to have a negative effect on real improvement. There is also a strong sense of personal accountability, and of responsibility for pupils' success, in the teaching profession which can be drawn upon to support concerted action for improvement. Governors, head-teachers and other school managers work with these forces, and need to use what is known about school improvement, and about what strategies are successful, in order to respond to the opportunities of the new freedom in creative and distinctive ways for each school.

The self managing institution

Over the last decade the education system of England and Wales has undergone a structural transformation, which has practical consequences for those who manage and govern schools. Schools, whether they are grant-maintained (GM), or funded by a local education authority (LEA), are now seen as self managing institutions. There are opportunities to determine aims and guiding principles for each school at a local level, in distinctive and diverse ways. Schools can select their own strategies for making progress towards their goals. Yet delegating responsibility to the level of the school does not diminish the importance of a collective national concern for the quality of publicly-funded education. All parents, teachers and those who make local and national policy for education have to be concerned with raising standards of achievement in all schools, so that all pupils benefit. The dilemma is that, while the potential of individual school and parental choice is explored as a means of raising standards, there has still to be some way of ensuring consistent quality in education across institutions.

One way of dealing with this dilemma is the growing practice of external, and internal, monitoring of results. The government has abdicated central control of the organisation of schools, but has chosen to prescribe more clearly than ever before what they must teach, and by what criteria they will be judged. It is intended that standards will be safeguarded by monitoring and evaluation of the work of schools from external and internal perspectives. These are seen to be means of bringing about local improvement, and of providing national education of high quality. External monitoring, particularly intended to provide information to parents, includes performance tables and external inspection. This public information creates pressures in schools, because of competition for pupils and funding. Some schools gain a good reputation, and gain pupils; others have to struggle with diminishing resources. Because of these very different circumstances internal monitoring is equally important as external publication of results. In advice to schools from the Department for Education and Employment (DFEE), and from the Office for Standards in Education (OFSTED), there is an equal emphasis on the need to evaluate school performance from within, and to use the findings to improve the quality of what is provided, and to enhance the achievements of pupils. School self-review, using such processes, can support the maintenance both of school autonomy and of national standards. Systems of school self-review provide both the means to improve, and the assurance that improvement is taking place. Figure 1 shows the virtuous circle of a planned approach to improvement in diagrammatic form – review leading to identifying targets for change, to action, to monitoring and modification of action, to meeting targets for improvement and to the setting of further targets as a result of the next review.

Figure 1 **A planned approach to improvement (1)**

In practice it is not at all simple to apply this wisdom to any individual school. The words monitoring and evaluation are often used as though their meaning was too obvious to question. Despite this, it can seem as though there is some mystery about managing change in this way, a mystery understood only by a select few. Friendly advisers can present the process as an instant cure for schools in difficulties: 'Are you doing monitoring and evaluation? What are your success criteria?' A headteacher may be challenged by inspectors working from OFSTED: 'How do you know what is happening in the classrooms? How do you know that your policies are being understood, are being implemented, are effective?'

Headteachers recognise these questions as appropriate, but also reserve the right to be sceptical and challenging in their turn. They need to be convinced that evaluation will work as a means of improving schools before they see it as a prime responsibility and find time for it to be carried out. The concept of monitoring and evaluation has to find a life outside the rhetoric of improvement, and must be taken from the realm of theory and tested in the day-to-day practice of schools. The responsibility of governors and school managers is to make their own sense of school self-review processes, a sense that fits the local situation for people and their needs in school. A school then needs to find the time to develop and apply its own system, and to discover whether it makes a difference.

School self-review has its roots in accountability, and in the responsibilities of schools to meet the needs of the communities where they are situated. It will develop its full value as schools use the freedom that has been given them to find a practical, relevant way of evaluation that neither paralyses people through too great a concern for the mechanisms of accountability, nor exhausts them with the burden of reactive responses to changing legislation from above.

The history of central influence

Over the last 30 years schools have been subject to a great deal of centrally inspired advice and organisational changes. The Newsom, Bullock and Cockcroft reports represent efforts to change the way pupils are taught by the presentation of evidence and informed advice, as do the publications on the curriculum from Her Majesty's Inspectors (HMI) in the late 1970s. The moves to comprehensive education (pursued with more or less emphasis depending on the government of the day) and the profound changes implied by the raising of the school leaving age and the introduction of CSE presented schools with unavoidable and urgent issues to manage.

Throughout this period there was a continuous and mounting concern about standards, explicitly introduced by James Callaghan when, as Prime Minister, he launched 'The Great Debate' in his speech at Ruskin College in 1976. Some believe that the freedom for professionals in schools to respond creatively to this concern has been eroded by legislative interference with the education profession, as in the Education Reform Act of 1988, which introduced the national curriculum, regular testing of pupils and local management of schools. Others would argue that the publicity given to failing schools and failing teachers as a result of the implementation of the 1992 Education Act, and the OFSTED inspection system, provides a much-needed further impetus for improvement.

Coopers & Lybrand, in a report commissioned by the Department for Education in 1988, effectively summarise the philosophy behind delegating finance to schools (local management):

> The underlying philosophy of financial delegation to schools stems from the application of the principles of good management. Good management requires the identification of management units for which objectives can be set and resources allocated; the unit is then required to manage itself within those resources in a way which seeks to achieve the objectives; the performance of the unit is monitored and the unit is held to account for its performance and for its use of funds.

> These concepts are just as applicable in the public sector as they are in the private sector.
>
> (Coopers & Lybrand, 1988)

But if public accountability, and choice for the consumers of education, were seen to provide pressure for good management, they were not by themselves deemed to be sufficient. What was missing from the 1988 legislation, according to the policy-makers, were clear lines of accountability, which would allow the maximum play of market forces and in this way promote the effective use of resources. Hence in 1992 and 1993 legislation was enacted to take the reforms one stage further, by introducing an external inspection service from OFSTED, regular public reports on schools, and a procedure for dealing with those schools that were found to be 'failing to provide an acceptable standard of education'.

Framework for the Inspection of Schools (OFSTED, 1995b) set standards by which schools should be judged, and has been itself a powerful influence on school management. The 1995 version of the *Framework* acknowledges the importance of school self-review procedures, and attempts to resolve the dilemma of the place of external and internal means of accountability. Used with confidence, the material in the *Framework* can help to raise the expectations of teachers about the conditions under which they work, and about their own opportunities to learn and develop. OFSTED stresses the partnership of external and internal evaluation when it states: 'The inspection process, feedback and reports give direction to the school's strategy for planning, review and improvement' (p 5) and 'Inspectors should consider the school's own priorities for development, evidence about the past attainments of pupils and any evidence from the school's own analysis of its provision and standards' (p 7).

Are delegated powers, coupled with increased measures of public accountability, all that is needed to improve standards in schools? Another dilemma for school managers is that it seems that something else is certainly required, at the school level. This something is personal, and interpersonal. It is about how people work together and generate confidence in their plans for change. It is what puts flesh on the bare bones of Figure 1. Improvement will only come about if changes happen in classrooms and between individuals. Legislation designed to apply 'good management practice' and 'social market principles' has almost entirely ignored the research and thinking that went on, internationally, throughout the 1970s and 1980s about what factors help a school to improve. These factors include the opportunity and motivation for individuals to reflect on their teaching and to collaborate in improving it.

School teachers, managers and governors now work in a system that expects an intelligent use of delegated powers, a willingness to focus on academic results as outcomes and the acceptance of external monitoring against national targets. Yet the climate created by successive pieces of legislation has been one in which those who work in schools feel both overburdened and undervalued. The freedom to exercise increased responsibility is there, but under the difficult conditions of low staff morale and reduced institutional funding. These conditions cannot be ignored and must be accepted consciously, but not obstructively, in working towards the selection of appropriate strategies for review and improvement.

School improvement in practice

Despite difficult conditions most of those who work in schools have an intuitive grasp of what really makes a school effective. They can gain some confidence to apply their intuition from accounts of successful improvement initiatives.

David Hargreaves and David Hopkins (1991) demonstrate that successful school improvement relies on four forces, all of which must be present in some measure and which must interact with each other. These are external, and internal, pressure and support. Without external pressure (for example an inspection, or expressions of parental dissatisfaction) a school may not move from 'its stable pattern of self-maintenance'. External pressure must be linked to internal pressure, coming from a recognition by governors, headteacher and senior staff of the advantages of any new development to the school itself. Conditions like this can lead to 'internal support', a release of self-help and self-directing energy. This may lead to the successful use of external support as part of a strategic partnership (e.g. with INSET providers and LEA advisers). Describing successful initiatives for change Hopkins and others (1994) assert that all of these forces can be seen in operation in schools that successfully manage change for improvement.

The new system of locally managed and self-governing (GM) schools provides the opportunity to be different. Many schools have responded by looking at how they are seen in the community, and by engaging in different forms of marketing. There are other ways in which this freedom can be used. There is a real opportunity to create a climate in the school that encourages and values the contribution individuals make. Successful schools are those that deliberately, and collaboratively, explore what happens in teaching, encourage mutual support and work towards broad agreement on educational values. A school like this sees itself as a learning organisation.

David Hargreaves argues for schools to use their freedom to manage in order to create learning organisations:

> Self management can be effective when the maintenance of the status quo suffices, but when the school has to manage itself in order to improve the quality of teaching and learning at the classroom level then the term learning organisation is a more accurate description of the kind of institution the school must become. For a school to become a learning organisation individual teachers must become learners, learning must be shared and learning must be institutionalised. This means putting in place mechanisms to help the school become a learning institution, and these mechanisms are still being discovered.
>
> (Hargreaves D, 1995)

As schools struggle with becoming learning organisations in reality, one of the first steps is to acknowledge the stresses that accountability has brought into teachers' lives. Personal stress and dissatisfaction are increased when external measures are applied in a way that appears insensitive.

What have been the effects of the new processes of external accountability on people who work in schools?

Which of the following have had a strong positive effect in your school? Which have been most negative? Which have had very little effect?

National Curriculum testing

Reporting to parents

National Curriculum key stage reporting

Publication of attendance figures

GCSE performance tables

External inspection

Governors' annual report to parents

Monitoring of school expenditure

Can you think of other procedures stressing accountability that have affected your school?

External accountability measures sometimes seem to divert, to frustrate, or even, at worst, to paralyse schools' own efforts to improve. Schools report that preparation for an OFSTED inspection can divert them from their own purposes for up to a year. There is a perception that techniques of publishing school league tables, and of open reporting on the strengths and weaknesses of schools as institutions, are intended not so much to ensure that schools will improve but to select them for growth or closure.

A primary headteacher in a school with 92 per cent bilingual pupils, speaking of performance tables at Key Stage 2, said:

> No matter how hard we work we're never going to come top of a league table. We know it is a real achievement to get so many children on Level 4 at Key Stage 2 when most did not even speak English in the nursery. League tables could affect the number of children, the budget allocation, the number of teachers and ultimately the quality of education we can offer. It's horrendous.
>
> (Primary school headteacher)

For consideration

What feelings have been aroused in your school about externally imposed accountability procedures?

Fear	Guilt	Satisfaction	Resentment
Hope	Celebration	Anger	Trust
Companionship	Despair	Suspicion	Confidence

What positive feelings can you build on?

What negative feelings must be faced and worked through?

How can you be sure that internal procedures generate less disabling feelings?

The headteacher quoted above works in a school which has made significant progress in raising the attainment of all the pupils, and can demonstrate this through results at Key Stages 1 and 2. She, and her staff, would agree that the members of their local community have a right to receive and interpret the information about the school's considerable achievements, and so join in its efforts to do better for the children who attend it. An element of public reporting is desirable, and perhaps is a duty that schools owe to the families who live around them.

A school should be able to take proper charge of its own improvement and reporting procedures, supporting those carrying out action and recognising achievement and success. Each school has to select its own response to the threat or opportunity of external evaluation. A new look at these apparent constraints may generate new ways of accommodating to them. Schools can look for ways of collaborating, of working in partnership with external inspection for instance. They can look for ways of minimising the negative impact of external publicity. Most importantly they should look for ways of ensuring that external methods complement and take account of the school's own systems for checking on its own success and planning for improvement.

What does the school believe about external accountability?

What information should local people have about the school?

Should the headings for reports to parents be chosen within the school?

Is there a place for nation-wide indicators?

What are the implications of the distortions caused by lack of agreement on a 'value added' model that genuinely takes account of community and resourcing differences?

Should parents set the agenda for the issues to be tackled in an inspection report and have a say before an evaluation is carried out?

How should the information about the school be collected?

Is there a place for external evaluators?

What is the value of an outside view?

Who should employ these evaluators – the school governors or the government?

How should information be passed on?

Can reporting be done in a clear and unambiguous manner?

Can the school explain the context of its rank order in league tables?

Are reports easy for members of the local community to obtain and to understand?

Who pays for translation into languages relevant to the area served by the school?

Using pressure and support

Acknowledging teachers' stress is undoubtedly one of the first steps a school must take, but there is a risk that for some schools it is also the last, because of suspicion, exhaustion or simply the lack of firm leadership. One skill of leadership is that of balancing pressure and support. A school which demonstrates confidence in its teachers can create a climate of collaboration and creativity where each person can contribute new ideas, and new energy, to the development of the school as a whole.

David Hargreaves (1994: p 55) stresses this possibility when he describes the key drivers for real changes and improvement in schools. He suggests that 'there are plenty of exciting ideas around; people just need the permission to support and try them so that the seeds germinate and flower... There has to be a way forward between utopian revolutions from above and defensive inertia from below.' Advice to schools comes thick and fast, and the courage to take an innovative route as a school and stick to it, despite the possibility of falling rolls and diminishing finances, or adverse reports from inspectors, is sometimes hard to find, and may even seem foolhardy. Planning, and the opportunity to modify plans in the light of feedback, can reduce this insecurity.

Open planning and open review procedures are the formal side of managing support. The school is required to set out its distinctive aims in its school prospectus. For many schools a revision of aims is a first step towards the next year's development plan. In the development plan the school will set out the immediate steps it intends to take to move towards its aims. Development planning has become an accepted practice, and is frequently used to manage internally inspired innovation and development. The school's responsibility for producing and working on an action plan following inspection provides a further opportunity for governors and managers to plan, albeit in response to external suggestions and requirements.

What is often lacking in planning is a feedback system that enables groups and individuals to know how they are doing and to make mid-plan changes. With the best will in the world those implementing a development plan, or action plan, may lose energy, or lose their way, during the course of a busy year. Keeping on track, firmly controlling the number of new initiatives, making sure that pupils are getting the best possible teaching in every classroom, are all serious and demanding issues for managers. Monitoring and reporting on progress towards targets that are specific to the plan, overall school self-review taking account of a wide range of views, and evaluation of new initiatives, are all ways to manage these issues. It is for each school to select the elements of monitoring and evaluation most appropriate to its context. A system of school self-review cannot be taken 'off the shelf' as standard; it must be chosen to fit the institution. Schools should select distinctive ways of improving from within.

Only teachers and the other adults who work in schools can bring about real change and improvement. To do this they need the informed support of governors, parents, children, local authority staff and even inspectors. They benefit from clear leadership that introduces new techniques and practices only when there are clear and meaningful reasons to do so. They need both the support and pressure referred to above, each in judicious measures. Their views need to be valued, and the freezing up of creativity sometimes caused by the imposition of accountability measures needs to be checked.

Some of the terms used in this book

School self-review and self-evaluation

Effective schools choose a range of processes, each applied in different ways, with the aim of knowing more about the school community in order to work better for the benefit of pupils. School self-review and school self-evaluation are phrases used to describe the blend of monitoring and evaluative procedures that may be adopted. The most important feature of any system is that it must make provision for acting on what is found out. It is argued in this book that each school needs its own system, each element of which has a clear purpose that is well understood by all involved at the time that it is applied. Important general principles have to be understood, but there is no unique way of applying them in any one institution.

Monitoring

Monitoring is a way of checking on the progress of the two aspects of planning discussed in the next chapter – maintenance and development. Through monitoring a school can check that both routine and new activities are proceeding as planned. Sometimes the verb 'monitor' is used to refer only to the collection of quantifiable data, measures of indicators related to school inputs, school processes and school outputs. In this book it is assumed that qualitative evidence may also be relevant to checking and monitoring. Measures are important, but so also are brief descriptions of progress on planned activities and changes.

Monitoring maintenance activities

This type of monitoring means checking year on year, and week by week, how the school is serving its pupils and its community. The success of the school will be monitored by the assessment of standards achieved by pupils, and through reporting on pupils' progress. Standard national performance indicators such as attendance rates, GCSE points scores and levels reached at different key stages will be used, as well as specific internal indicators. Routine activities about which there has been agreement among teachers, such as the setting and marking of homework, or the amount of time given to reading in primary classes, can also be monitored.

Monitoring planned developments

Each year a school may plan to do new things, introducing changes that relate to hoped for improvements. In this context monitoring will be used to check that the action is proceeding as planned. Monitoring can be a source of support (and pressure) for the person with responsibility for the action, and it can be useful in verifying that the resources allocated are adequate and are, in reality, being used to support the work. Feedback from monitoring can be used to make ongoing work more satisfying, more manageable and more useful.

Evaluation

Evaluation goes more deeply into the purpose and value of activities. It is a planned process making a systematic study of the quality of provision. It involves more than the collection of information, though obtaining evidence is one important part of the systematic process. In performing an evaluation information has to be analysed and interpreted to make judgements about the nature, impact and value of the provision being studied. Evaluation should have an effect on future decisions; the judgements made need to be reported and acted upon.

Evaluation of the quality of the work of the school
The description above highlights three things about evaluation: it should provide information about the quality of what the school is providing and hence focus on the outcomes not the action; it should use a range of methods for collecting evidence; it should be used to back up decisions.

Evaluation, in going more deeply into the effects of action, can be useful in helping people to make decisions about changing their published plans. Evaluation is also a way of acknowledging publicly the effects of any unplanned action that had unstated objectives, yet brought about some significant change or improvement. Evaluation can help sustain the work of a school through

- celebration of success;
- provision of reasons to justify a change of plan;
- acknowledgement of the range of action that is going on;
- improvement of future planning and action.

Selective evaluation of action in relation to objectives

It is recommended in this book that some of the action set out in planning is subject to more in-depth evaluation. Because of the time needed to do a thorough job of evaluation it is necessary to be selective. It will be important to set objectives at the same time as planning action, in order to examine the outcomes that are linked to the objectives. For example, a whole range of activities might be set up in a primary school to bring about better home/school links and more parental involvement in children's learning. Without a clear statement of objectives at the beginning it is possible that the 'busyness' of the action takes over. The planned events and schemes may happen, but no considered evaluation of the intended effect takes place. If there is planned evaluation of features that are defined initially some judgement can be made about the worth of what has been done.

For consideration

School self-review

The OFSTED *Framework* (1995b) expresses certain expectations about aspects of monitoring and evaluation that should be in use in a school.

1   Monitoring whole school targets

e.g. in examination success, attendance rates

Does your school have such targets? How frequently are they monitored? What is analysed and published?

2   Monitoring individual pupils' progress

Who is principally responsible for monitoring individual pupils' progress? What is the prime purpose? To what extent are pupils involved?

3   Monitoring individual teachers in their classrooms

Is there formal monitoring of the work of teachers? By whom? Informal monitoring? What is done about what is found out?

4   Monitoring progress on the school development plan and action plans

How do you keep track of the pace of action? How do you monitor the effects? Can you recall making changes in the course of a year as a result of monitoring?

5   Evaluation of the quality of the work of the school

To what extent would you say that you have internal self review procedures?

6   Evaluation of action (innovation) in relation to objectives

Have you evaluated the effects of any innovation recently, perhaps for outside funding bodies, or for governors?

Do you have any thoughts about the use of the words **monitoring**, **evaluation**, **school review** in advice from OFSTED? Is there a need for definitions and consistency? What words or phrases do you use in your school?

2 Planning at all levels

• •

Planning procedures are the formal side of managing support. The school is required to publish its distinctive aims in its prospectus. In the development plan the school will set out the immediate steps it intends to take to move towards its aims.

This chapter is about planning in school, and the relationship between planning and self-review, monitoring and evaluation. It sets out some of the purposes of planning, and examines the relationship between the planned and the unplanned, between the innovation and the maintenance activities that go on in a school. It prompts consideration of what makes sense for the individual school, and illustrates this by a closer look at planning for curriculum and staff development.

Purposes of school development planning

Development planning for schools became widespread in the mid 1980s, with the allocation of staff development funding to schools. A plan was required from the school in order for funds to be delegated, and such plans were required to have targets whose achievement could be monitored. The continuation of funding was dependent on schools being able to demonstrate an effective use of the delegated funds. LEAs required schools to produce whole school staff development plans, and evaluations, for funds related to in-service training. Because plans were a new concept, and seen to be imposed from outside, only rarely did they have a significant effect on the work of the school as a whole. However, they provided many schools with their first models of development planning.

After the Education Reform Act of 1988 LEAs were required to delegate a large proportion of their education budgets through formula allocation to individual schools. The school development plan was widely promoted as the right way for schools to go about managing their devolved funding, with guidance from sources such as Coopers & Lybrand (1988), and Caldwell and Spinks' s (1988) description of self managing schools in Tasmania. Since then there has been a period of some confusion, with the term 'development plan' used to describe a number of types of documents.

In some schools (especially primary schools), where the introduction of school development planning coincided with the introduction of the national curriculum, the school development plan began life as a curriculum development plan, perhaps merged with a staff development plan. In some secondary schools, in contrast, the development plan was primarily a financial management plan, related to those elements of the budget that were seen to be disposable after core or base requirements had been met. Some LEAs provided an approved format for the school development plan, and expected schools to submit their plans to the education office. One of the problems for schools has been that the variety of types of plan, and of purposes for planning, have not always been sufficiently acknowledged and discussed. The following set of purposes for planning was created through discussion in a group of headteachers from all phases. School planning, they agreed, is intended

- to establish clarity of purpose;
- to give all parties an opportunity for involvement and ownership;
- to give a structure to development;
- to manage change rather than react to it;
- to focus energies more specifically;
- to ensure that resources are used to the best advantage;
- to lessen the strain of overwhelming demands;
- to enable the school to measure progress.

Figure 2 shows some of the processes of planning associated with these purposes.

Figure 2 **Processes of planning**

Aims

Indicating what the school is trying to achieve.

Establishing a baseline against which the school can evaluate the success of its activities.

Audit

Considering evidence from evaluation which has reviewed the curriculum, staffing, premises and equipment, links with parents and the community and staff development in terms of

- maintaining existing practice;
- supporting on-going development;
- identifying areas for new development and growth.

Resource implications

Considering staffing, equipment, premises, INSET, time and finance.

Selecting priorities

Identifying and agreeing a manageable number of priorities for the coming year.

Preserving a balance between maintenance and development activities.

Action planning

Writing plans which describe how programmes of work are to be undertaken.

Financial statement

Allocating funds to support agreed priorities.

Review and evaluation

Regular progress checks against criteria agreed in the school, providing the opportunity to support action and information for the audit stage of new planning.

Formulating a school development plan

Recent advice on development planning for governors (DFE, 1995a) positively links school improvement and the development plan, advising the governors to set their strategy through the plan, and stating that 'knowing the school's current performance provides a basis for improvement'. A plan should include targets for development over the next few years and a statement of how the school will meet them.

Governors are advised that the development plan should be based on wide consultation, and it should above all focus on raising standards of achievement and on the quality of pupils' learning. The role of the governing body is to provide overall direction and criticism, and to review the plan regularly. The plan should be based on simple questions such as:

- where are we trying to get to?
- where are we now?
- how can we get from where we are now to where we want to be?
- what are the key priorities?
- have we got the resources to do it?
- who is responsible for doing what and by when?
- how will we know if we have achieved our goals?

One model for writing a school development plan illustrates how the answers to these specific questions can be displayed. After identifying its priorities, the school community needs to clarify exactly what it wants to achieve in these areas, and to express this in the form of specific **objectives**, which are linked to intended **outcomes**, to be arrived at by using certain **strategies**. The strategies lead to **action plans** which are working documents for different groups in the school. In this model the terminology is simply defined.

Definitions

An **objective** indicates the state or condition to be achieved. Within a specific area of activity targeted for development it is a description of an improved situation in a minimum number of words.

An **outcome** (or **target**) is a result or consequence of the strategy being employed to achieve the stated objective. Outcomes incorporate the reasons why a particular objective has been chosen, i.e. what will be seen that indicates that improvement has taken place. They must be observable, and possibly measurable. There may be a number of outcomes for each objective and in each case they should be easy to verify.

A **strategy** implies a set of actions designed to help achieve the stated outcomes. A strategy is usually one of several answers to the question 'What can I/we most usefully do to achieve the objective?'

An **action plan** contains a more detailed specification for the implementation of individual strategies. Action plans show who will do what, when it will be done, the resources required and the methods to be used in evaluation and reporting. Action plans are at the very least a list of **tasks** (DES, 1989), but are more than this because they include a link to the outcomes, through defining a reporting framework. Tasks follow from strategies as the strategies are broken down into action planning steps.

For the purposes of monitoring it is important that a timescale is given for the action, and that it is set out in a series of manageable steps.

An illustration of the relationship between objectives, outcomes and strategies is set out in Figure 3.

Figure 3 **Relationship between objectives, outcomes and strategies**

Objective	Outcomes	Strategies
To develop effective school discipline	*The school environment is safe, caring and orderly.* *Students are self-disciplined.* *Student learning is not interrupted by irresponsible behaviour.* *Teaching is not interrupted by irresponsible behaviour.*	*Develop a discipline policy in partnership with students and their families.* *Develop and maintain a success oriented environment.*

Using a plan

What is important is to make sense, in schools at a day-to-day level, of the general and theoretical principles laid down by outside experts. A framework must allow for individual differences between schools, and also embody general principles of clarity, manageability and the involvement of all. In using such a framework for planning many schools have found that the greatest challenge has been to establish criteria for the success of their plans, and have recognised the need to develop their ability to do this in a meaningful way. Criteria, like indicators of performance, have a simple function. They should be selected principally to enable the school to keep a shared sense of direction, and to use knowledge of progress, or lack of it, to help keep the school on its own chosen track. An important purpose of planning is 'to enable the school to measure progress'. Governors are asked to consider the question 'How will we know if we have achieved our goals?' There is a common assumption that a central purpose of planning, as of school self-review, is maintaining and improving the quality of education provided. In principle, then, there should be a strong link between planning and self-review; in practice it has been one of the more neglected elements of planning. Some practical guidance will be found in Chapters 3, 4 and 5 of this book, and School Planning Sheet 3 on page 203 in particular supports a link between planning and monitoring.

For consideration

What is your development plan for?
- because the LEA/OFSTED may wish to see it?
- to manage a reduction in resources as effectively as possible?
- to make sure all the staff and governors understand school priorities?
- to link curriculum and staff development?
- to control the pace of the introduction of national initiatives?
- to see how well the school is doing what it set out to do?

What other purposes does the development plan serve?

Planned and unplanned innovation

Before looking in more detail at how 'monitoring and evaluation' can be built in to the plan there is a need to clear up some questions, or at least recognise that there is some confusion and agree to leave them as unresolved issues. Is there a clear enough distinction between maintenance and developments or innovations? What needs to be written down in the plan? Is there a danger, in relying on planning, that unplanned innovations will not be recognised and evaluated? Is there, on the other hand, a risk that the everyday processes of the school (the maintenance activities) are not properly costed, described, evaluated and celebrated?

In the 1970s and early 1980s whole-school self-review processes such as GRIDS (Guidelines for Review and Internal Development in Schools) aimed to review those elements of a school's processes that seemed important to those working in them. In this way they were unlikely to omit issues that were subjectively seen as of concern. However, they have been criticised for being sometimes defensive, and for not tackling issues central to the process of teaching and learning sufficiently critically. They enabled schools to be selective (in the issues they focused on), which is realistic, but were often not related to resources. Their strength lay in the involvement of many people in the review process, a 'bottom-up' approach. A more objective alternative is to relate evaluation to predetermined targets, set out in the development plan.

A balance has to be found between the more subjective and the more objective approaches. A criticism of a system of evaluation that relies too much on the planning process, and on targets set out in the plan, is that it can also be unduly limiting in another way. It can leave out the unplanned innovations, some of which are central factors in improvement. It can omit evaluation of the day-to-day maintenance activities, for instance classroom teaching. What can be learned from past experience is that, whatever method is used, it is important to focus evaluation on activities that make a real difference to standards, and that it is important to sustain progress through subsequent action.

In effective school planning and self-review there needs to be some means of considering the whole range of activities that a school engages in, whether they are in the plan or not. If, in a particular school, the written development plan is about development and innovation, there is probably an unwritten 'maintenance plan' which ensures that the school keeps running. If, on the other hand, plans are written to cover all the aspects of school organisation, and to try to account for the way the whole budget is spent, they can become bureaucratic and unwieldy, and no one will refer to them. Most plans make some compromise. Often important things happen in the school that are not in the plan. This should only be a cause for concern if decisions about managing resources are made with no reference to planning.

Figure 4 shows how the consideration of the questions 'what is planned? what is unplanned? what is new? what is ongoing?' can throw light on what needs to be reviewed. After those managing a school have considered the distinctions illustrated in Figure 4 it may be decided that too much innovation takes place outside the 'official' plan. It may be revealed that the maintenance or development that is written into the plan is too often affected by innovations introduced from within or imposed from outside. In planning to use monitoring and evaluation for improvement all of these factors need to be examined and taken into account.

Figure 4 **Innovation or maintenance? Planned or unplanned?**

	In the School Development Plan	**Done**	**NOT in the School Development Plan**	**Done**
Innovation and development	*Devise and use assessment records related to weekly planning*	✓	*Class trip with parents to country park*	✓
Maintenance	*Staff training with new graphics software*		*Key Stage assessment*	✓
			Parents' consultation evenings	✓

A new variety of plan is emerging, inspired partly by post-OFSTED action plans and partly by advice given about school improvement and school effectiveness. This type of school plan focuses on areas which are specifically targeted for improvement; perhaps it should be called a school improvement plan. It is likely to make provision for evaluation. In devising a system of self-review, however, other aspects of the school's work must also be recognised.

Conflicting advice is confusing if left unexamined, but in practice it is possible to live with the ambiguity once we have acknowledged it. Each school should analyse its own development plan and process of planning, and seek to make them meet the school's own needs without being unduly bureaucratic. Advice about forms of planning should be accepted only when it will make a distinct improvement to what already goes on in the school, and where the reasons for change are clear. Changes to development planning may arise from considerations of school self-review. Review and planning are interlinked. Creativity may be lost if they are linked too rigidly or too formally.

For consideration

The school's development plan may have elements of maintenance and development.

Can you answer these questions about it?

- does it serve your purpose?
- are the targets you intend to achieve sufficiently clear?
- can you check on what it costs to implement?
- do you have means of using feedback to make alterations to the plan within its lifetime?
- can you take account of the effect of any unplanned actions?

In the light of your answers what changes, if any, would be worth making to the format of the plan?

Two areas of planning which have a strong part to play in the improvement of schools are curriculum and staff development. In the following sections these two important elements are examined to provide practical illustrations of some of the issues of this chapter.

Planning curriculum development

Secondary schools

In secondary schools curriculum planning is very often delegated to departments. Much of the teaching of the curriculum will follow a maintenance pattern, where only changes to examination syllabuses are seen to require any specific planning. The department policy and scheme of work provide the basis for maintenance, and are the means by which departments try to get good and consistent teaching of the subject. This can mean, however, that school targets for improving pupils' performance in examinations seem unrelated to the curriculum planning in each subject. The school's planning and review process needs to bridge this gap in some way.

Departments are often asked to produce their action plans for a year, or for the longer term. Sometimes heads of department and their colleagues are unclear what purpose these are intended to serve. A department action plan can be used to set out the timescale for reviewing the scheme of work, perhaps focusing on a year group or a key stage. It can set out a bid for increased resources, to support a specific innovation in teaching methods or in curriculum coverage. It should include an element concentrating on specific improvements in teaching, and about the department's strategy to raise the standards pupils achieve in the subject.

Primary schools

In primary schools there is likely to be a subject adviser or manager in the school for each national curriculum subject. The roles that these people have are not always clear, and their influence is limited in practice by the facts that they have very little time to undertake the tasks, and that they often have multiple responsibilities. Especially at pre-Key Stage 1 and Key Stage 1, much of the medium and short term planning will be done by a team of teachers of children of that age group.

The most effective practice is where a designated member of staff acts as curriculum leader for one or more subjects, and the school plan sets out a rolling review of the success of teaching and learning in different curriculum areas. All staff participate, led by the person who has specifically developed their own knowledge and expertise for a particular subject. In small schools this review can only be undertaken at a relatively gentle pace.

As in secondary schools the 'maintenance' aspect of curriculum planning will be set out in the policy and scheme of work. This may be seen to need review or improvement, and someone must have overall responsibility for leading other teachers in this task. The school development plan can set out the timescale for such review and improvement.

Long term and medium term planning for class teaching will be written down, but not usually in the school development plan. Specific improvements in teaching a subject (for example a school-wide focus on numeracy designed to improve children's success in mathematics) should be in the development plan, and should be equally important as routine curriculum planning.

Planning staff development (teachers and associate staff)

The staff development plan should co-ordinate individual professional training needs with the development needs of the school. It should also have a link with the outcomes of appraisal. The school has to have a means of ensuring that the limited resources for staff development are targeted at the right people, those who have a need to extend their professional skills, and those who are committed to working with colleagues to share what they have learned. The sources of funding for staff development have led to the professional development of teaching staff receiving the most attention. An emerging national emphasis on the continuous professional development of all staff, often associated with initiatives such as Investors in People, is an important reminder of the need to consider the contribution of all who work in schools and how their work can be supported.

There should be direct links with curriculum planning. For example, in a primary school, staff development funds might be used for all members of staff to improve their teaching of art and design through a practical course. The staff development plan should support school improvement initiatives. It could, for example, provide for a staff training day for everyone to learn more about ways of effectively teaching children of different abilities in the same class. Where there are such links it should be possible to evaluate the training in terms of its practical effects. These planning links should also be used to ensure that the school sustains professional development activities, so that they are not merely associated with an INSET day or a course, but have some other roots in the school.

The staff development plan should enable all available resources for in-service training to be used in a way that is determined by the school. Needs should be identified in the school, so that activities and providers may be chosen selectively, not merely used because of an advertisement seen by chance. Ultimately the effects of staff development should be capable of being evaluated in terms of observable improvements to teaching and learning.

Further considerations for planning

Planning has been recommended as the proper basis for running a school, and monitoring and evaluation are a logical consequence. There are, however, pitfalls in trying to manage an educational institution of creative professional people with too much emphasis on the planned and the measurable.

For consideration

Are you
- planning to do too much?
- planning to innovate with too few resources?
- confusing people by introducing too many varieties of plan?
- leaving no space for unplanned improvisation?
- creating a 'them and us' mentality, those who believe in the plan and those who are more cynical?

- draining energy through not acknowledging and publicising progress?
- failing to use reporting and review to keep on track or change direction?

The development plan is sometimes likened to the map of a journey. Realistically, in a school, there will be different views about where to go. One deputy headteacher in a school which was developing its improvement strategies spoke of those who 'still wanted to go to Bridlington' while the rest of the staff were 'setting off for Barbados'. He commented that they would send them a postcard. Circumstances change, and successful action changes people's views. Sharing the outcomes of planning is like a metaphorical postcard saying 'wish you were here'.

Continuing with the metaphor of a journey, the action and commitment of some can be seen as the fuel to keep things moving. Monitoring checks the fuel gauge and the speedometer, and may force decisions about buying more fuel or keeping up the pace. Monitoring also checks the map against the route. Only evaluation checks whether you like where you have got to, and whether it is anything like you imagined and hoped it would be when you set out. Evaluation may perhaps lead to a change in direction, a redirection of energy, or, when things have gone well, to a celebratory announcement and congratulations to those who have worked hard to get there.

For consideration

Planning and evaluation

In what ways do you allocate resources?

Time? Support staff? Books and materials? Training?

Can resources be redirected if monitoring shows the need?

In what ways do you allocate responsibilities?

Are responsibilities within the plan always linked to roles in school? If not, have those leading action been given sufficient power?

How do you support those responsible?

How do you monitor their work?

In what ways do you measure success?

Who sets the objectives for each part of the plan?

Do these objectives make sense to all involved? (pupils and parents?)

Is there freedom from jargon?

Are there school standard key indicators (e.g. successes at Key Stage assessments)?

Are you using reporting arrangements (to staff, to parents, to governors) to publicise success?

3 Monitoring the work of the school

Monitoring is a way of checking on the progress of two aspects of planning – maintenance and development. Through monitoring a school can check that both routine and new activities are proceeding as planned.

This chapter deals with aspects of monitoring the work of the school in order to check year by year, and week by week, how the school is serving its pupils and its community. Assessment of standards achieved by pupils and reporting on pupils' progress form part of the monitoring of the success of the school. The expectation that a school will set targets in order to measure its improvement is discussed. Routine maintenance activities can also be monitored, as can development activities, in order to check that the action is proceeding as planned. Monitoring can lead to modifications that make ongoing work more satisfying, and more useful.

Approaches to school improvement

There are two apparently opposing approaches to school improvement, the rational approach which stresses targets and systems, and the creative approach which stresses ownership and personal motivation. The dilemma for school managers is to use both of these, with a judicious balance that fits the situation in the school.

The rational approach

The rational approach to school improvement (see Figure 1 on page 20) stresses the need to set targets and to monitor progress. OFSTED's process for inspecting schools is an example of the application of this model. In the inspection system the remedy for weaknesses in provision and achievement is seen as the application of scientific principles. These state that the gap between performance and requirements must be identified, and the steps to close that gap set out in an action plan. The steps must be followed and progress monitored. Targets are set, and success is measured in terms of the achievement of these targets.

Inspectors' judgements about schools demonstrate expectations based on this model. Early findings, from secondary and primary schools, judged there to be inadequate monitoring procedures in over half the schools inspected

(OFSTED, 1995a). Weaknesses were particularly apparent when monitoring was being carried out without impacting on achievements or standards, and without addressing issues. Inspectors reported that school managers rarely set standards for institution-wide practice in planning, teaching and assessment. They found that monitoring and evaluation of the learning of pupils, and of the outcomes of teaching, were weak features of many schools.

Such an emphasis on the importance of monitoring can make it seem like an ideal and unproblematic solution to raising standards. The danger with over-reliance on this theory of improvement is that it can be like some forms of dieting. The target can be achieved, but maybe no real and lasting change in behaviour takes place. Consequently the changes do not endure, and the effort to meet the targets has been misdirected and wasted.

The rational approach summarised above should not be rejected out of hand, however. What is particularly helpful is the way it focuses on outcomes, for instance the attainment of individual pupils, or the aggregated examination successes of cohorts of pupils from the school.

The creative approach

Some schools prefer an approach that places attitudes, feelings and ways of working collaboratively at the heart of any improvement process. Such approaches have focused on the important component of 'ownership' of change projects, and have stressed the individual's creative contribution to teaching and learning in the school. The risk in employing these strategies alone is that there may be no change at all in terms of pupils' success, but only a generalised sense of feeling better, with a tenuous link with school improvement.

A synthesis

Schools cannot afford to ignore either of these perspectives. In Chapter 6 of this book the place of people's attitudes and feelings will be examined more closely, in the light of what will be presented in this chapter and Chapters 4 and 5, to support elements of the rational approach. It is important not to fall into the trap of setting rational and creative approaches up against each other as polarised opposites; after all that is not how we work as human beings. Without continuous monitoring of what is happening to individual teachers and pupils in the classroom there is a danger that projects and plans can become entirely theoretical, a sort of 'window-dressing'. And once an institution adopts some form of monitoring, this can support the reflective processes of creative individuals who are enabled to observe themselves and others acting, and to think about what they are doing at a conscious and shared level. Reflection, reinforced by monitoring, can change a situation enough to provide ideas for the next stage of action.

It is not always easy to convince people who work in a school that monitoring some aspects of their work will make a real contribution to improving what they do. The best advice is to start small, and to build on accepted processes. If an aspect of monitoring is to be introduced or extended there are several questions that should be asked.

For consideration

Questions about monitoring
- why are we going to do this?
- what are we monitoring?
- how will we collect evidence?
- what are we going to do about what we find out?
- will it make enough difference to be worth the effort?

The answer to the first of these questions is the most important. It should also provide the answer to the fourth question: 'what are we going to do about what we find out?' Although it may be possible to answer the fifth question only after trying something out, it is important not to omit it.

The role of governors in monitoring

Governors and headteachers are expected to know how well the school is performing. They have different levels of 'need to know'. According to DFE advice (1995a) governors should focus on where they can add most value to the work of the school. It is acknowledged that they have important powers and duties, but only limited time and resources. The advice suggests that ' a school's review of its own effectiveness should be a part of its planning and review cycle' and 'an important role for the governing body is to monitor the work of the school'. Governing bodies need to decide which are the key indicators they should monitor, who will provide the information and when it should be received.

Governing bodies' responsibilities and actions

Governors should

- decide the school's strategy for improvement, and check on its progress;
- be answerable to the wider local community for their work and the work of the school.

They do this by

- keeping the framework for running the school under review;

- receiving regular reports from the headteacher and other staff;
- asking challenging questions.

The more knowledge the governors gain about the way the school works, the more they may become concerned that they should know about everything that is going on in the school. This is not practically possible, nor is it appropriate. It can lead to overload and increased anxiety for everyone. It is important for the governing body to be selective about what it seeks to monitor at any one time. A strategy for monitoring has to be discussed and agreed.

For example, one group of governors worked together to appoint a new headteacher, after the resignation of a long-serving head. During this process they discovered that they did not know as much as they thought they should about things that had been going on in the school. Their concern could have led to the new headteacher having no freedom to operate and to manage the school. They were advised to select no more than two key areas of innovation to monitor in depth, over one year, and to supplement this by requiring regular reports on work in different subjects, including the standards achieved. Placing these reports as regular items on their agendas, or those of sub-committees, also helped to ensure that their time was used as they felt best, and that they were not swamped by agenda items originating from outside the school.

Having gained information in this way, the governors need to think about how their knowledge can be applied for the school's benefit. Informally they can ask more pertinent and challenging questions; more formally they can set new targets in collaboration with teachers; and, finally, they should be able to make decisions about the allocation of finance to new initiatives and to maintenance activities, with reference to need and to the likelihood of success.

Managing monitoring processes with the governors

For consideration

How do the governors obtain information about...

- examination and test results?
- the school's achievement in relation to achievement in previous years?
- the school's performance in comparison with that of other schools, nationally and locally?
- the improvement in achievement levels of pupils throughout their time at school (the 'value added')?
- performance in different subject areas and at different key stages?
- the progress made by different groups of pupils, for instance pupils grouped by gender, ethnic background or level of prior attainment?
- attendance?
- applications for admission?
- destinations of those who leave?

How do the governors learn about...
- staff morale and commitment?
- the staff as a resource, and the way they are deployed?
- the level of satisfaction of parents and the community?
- the appropriateness of the school's curriculum?
- pupils' behaviour?
- pupils' attitudes to learning?
- the effectiveness of spending the school's budget allocation?

The most important characteristic for a school to develop, and for governors to support, is the capacity to improve from within. Self knowledge is needed; the power of any external intervention is limited, and should be focused on generating a school's capacity for sustainable self-renewal.

Managing a realistic timetable for both monitoring and evaluation is important, and School Planning Sheet 1, shown partially completed on page 200, provides a way of recording what the school has committed itself to, and of sharing this knowledge in a concise form with the governing body. It can give an overview of aspects of monitoring described in this chapter, and of the application of evaluation processes set out in Chapters 4 and 5.

The headings in the first row, 'areas of school life', may be varied from year to year, and will be used selectively as appropriate. Monitoring targets are set out in the second row and might include such indicators as examination successes, exclusion and attendance rates, use of library and other resources to support learning. The features to be evaluated will be selected as part of the process described in Chapter 4. These are more qualitative indicators such as, for instance, pupils' engagement in learning, or the involvement of parents. Evidence will be collected by appropriate procedures selected from those in Chapter 5. Completion of School Planning Sheet 1 with reporting dates (row 5) and levels of future planning (row 6) should ensure that the processes of monitoring and evaluation are not sterile exercises, but have a proper influence on decisions and action. As the partially completed example of School Planning Sheet 1 shows, it is an overview for governors, and leaves much detail to be worked through by groups in the school.

The next sections of this chapter describe four applications of monitoring, relating to whole school targets, to individual pupils' achievement, to the work of teachers in the classroom and to monitoring progress on development and action plans.

Monitoring whole school targets for academic achievement

One principal motivating factor for setting targets about school performance as a whole is the government's introduction of school league tables and public reporting. As one of its promises to parents in the Parent's Charter (DFE, 1994) the government introduced annual comparative performance tables for secondary schools. Governing bodies of both secondary and primary schools are also required to publish certain information in each year's school prospectus. The government's main objective is to ensure that parents choosing from among local schools, and keeping in touch with the schools their children attend, have ready access to up-to-date factual information. As a school chooses its own targets and indicators to monitor, it will take account of the measures of performance that are required nationally. These are summarised in Figures 5 and 6.

Figure 5   **Indicators made public in performance tables for secondary schools**

GCSE performance

The percentage of 15-year-olds (i.e. all pupils in their final year of schooling) gaining

(i) 5 or more grades A* to C (ii) 5 or more grades A* to G (iii) 1 or more grades A* to G.

Vocational qualifications pre-16

The percentage of 15-year-olds, studying for relevant vocational qualifications or units, who succeed in obtaining all those qualifications or units.

Advanced level point scores

The average point score per exam entry of pupils (16, 17 and 18) entered for at least 1 A, or AS equivalent level.

The average point scores at A level (i) of pupils (16, 17 and 18) entered for fewer than 2 GCSE A levels or AS equivalent level and (ii) of pupils (16, 17 and 18) entered for 2 or more GCSE A levels or AS equivalent level.

Vocational qualifications post-16

The percentage of 16,86 17 or 18 year olds, in the final year of specified advanced vocational qualifications, achieving those qualifications.

Attendance

Percentage of half days missed due to unauthorised absence.

Figure 6 **Indicators made public in the school prospectus**

For secondary schools

The results of pupils who are 15 at the beginning of the school year, in GCSE by subject; this listing must include English, mathematics and science.

The results of those studying for vocational qualifications or units.

The GCSE results separately for boys, girls and all pupils, in percentages as for the performance tables, set against comparative figures for all schools in England.

The results of pupils at A and AS levels by subject.

The A level points score (set out in two tables – those taking fewer than 2 subjects and those taking 2 or more), by sex, set against comparative figures for all schools in England.

Results of National Curriculum tests of 14-year-olds.

Details of routes taken by pupils over 16.

Rates of authorised and unauthorised absence.

For primary schools
Results of National Curriculum tests for 7 and 11-year-olds.
Rates of authorised and unauthorised absence.

Although the prime purpose for publishing these indicators is to inform parents and support their right to choose, use can be made of them at the school level. One opportunity is that of making comparisons between the school's own performance and that of other schools, just as parents do. Concern has been expressed that parents will get the wrong impression from national league tables, if they are unaware of the context the school operates in, for instance the level of achievement on entry, the social background or proficiency in English of the pupils. Schools too need to be sure that they are comparing like with like. Ways of measuring school performance that take account of the level of attainment of pupils on entry are known as 'value added' measures. The government has accepted the importance of acknowledging the value added by a school, and has commissioned a number of studies (DFE, 1995b).

The Secretary of State for Education has made a commitment to the principle that measures of value added by schools and colleges should be included in the performance tables in due course. These measures will be chosen so as to be both reliable and intelligible to the readers, and also fairly simple to collect so that the process is not overly burdensome for schools and colleges. The Labour Party (1995) also proposes an improvement to the performance tables, using both value added measures and comparisons with a school's previous performance. In order to use this information as part of a strategy to raise standards, schools would be required to set targets for improvement based upon their previous best performance, and would use baseline testing, for instance of 5-year-olds as they enter compulsory schooling, to make the setting of targets more precise.

A second opportunity, for schools, which arises from the introduction of public measures of performance is that there is a better framework for looking at comparative year-by-year improvements within a school. The Performance Indicators in Primary Schools (PIPS) project, based at Durham University, can provide primary schools with value added scores for each pupil in Years 2 and 6, and with graphs that show the school's own value added scores in comparison with other schools. Since the start of the project in 1993 those schools involved have benefited from the experience of the development of value added measures which rely on assessments made in the school. At secondary level the National Consortium for Examination Results has investigated and applied a 'pupil-referenced' analysis to GCSE results. This sort of analysis does not provide a basis for comparisons between schools, but does give important information for an individual school about the comparative successes of subject departments, and about improvements over a period of years. In Nottinghamshire LEA a scheme (DFEE, 1996) is used which enables pupils and departments to make comparisons between performance in different subjects. In addition many schools are using pupil-referenced measures applied to A level and GCSE scores to monitor the school's overall performance from year to year (DFE, 1995c).

Pupil-referenced measures are the most detailed source of information. A school may choose, on the other hand, simply to monitor the changes in its indicators in the national performance table as a basis for measuring improvement. In this case it is preferable to use some device such as three-year rolling averages, in order to minimise the effect of the differences between year cohorts on intake.

A third opportunity for a school is to monitor its contribution to national targets. A school can look at how those young adults who have formerly been pupils have performed in terms of national benchmarks, such as National Targets for Education and Training.

Fourthly, the school may wish to target and review the performance of particular groups of pupils, perhaps boys and girls if there appears to be a significant variation in achievement between the sexes, or the achievement of pupils for whom English is not the home language. In making its own selection of indicators the school will want to decide what information is most useful, and what knowledge most likely to influence action for change. Data about examination and assessment success can be published graphically in informative ways, with appropriate use of information technology. It is not discriminatory to hold data on different ethnic groups, or to compare the performance of boys and girls in English. It is important information for teachers to have and to discuss. It has been found that when data is used to make comparisons and presented to schools by outsiders, for instance by inspectors, the reaction is often defensiveness and the findings may be discounted as atypical. Only regular comparisons made and discussed within the school will have any real effect on planning.

By themselves indicators cannot give a full picture of the operation of a school. They may, however, give advance warning of areas where management attention is required; and they can also indicate how well the school is moving towards its objectives. Targets and objectives in this sense are there, as are the national targets, for an institution to aspire to; they do not work as planning targets do in providing information about action itself. Some of the school's own targets should be selected to relate to collective academic success, however, in order to avoid becoming submerged in a large number of poorly focused initiatives for improvement. Effective planning for improvement includes setting realistic, challenging and measurable targets.

Monitoring individual pupils' progress

This aspect of monitoring is familiar in all schools, partly because of the requirement for national curriculum assessment, and partly because of the growth of school initiatives linked to recording of achievement. These two influences represent different ends of the spectrum of views about the effect of monitoring on individual achievement. National curriculum assessment, at the extreme, can be characterised as an assessment against externally imposed criteria, where there is no negotiation about the application of these standards and where there is no need to pass on the judgement to the person being judged, nor any expectation that this person would be involved in their own assessment. The recording achievement initiative, on the other hand, has developed with the characteristics of self-assessment, noting achievements that are valued and understood by the person making them, and making a clear link to future endeavours and aspirations.

Having been subject to both these influences, many schools are in a good position to apply the best of both styles to monitoring pupils' achievement. On the one hand a knowledge of attainment can lead to good planning for the next steps of learning, and on the other hand an honest appraisal of past achievements, present weaknesses and future targets can lead to the active involvement of the learner in working for improvement. Imaginatively introduced procedures can help a school raise individual and collective standards of achievement.

One school's response to an OFSTED key issue 'the school should take action to improve standards' was to extend and develop a range of strategies for monitoring pupils' achievements and for involving pupils and parents in looking at their successes and weaknesses. One year on from the introduction of their post-OFSTED action plan the headteacher wrote to parents to tell them:

To encourage even greater achievement we have

- improved our 'merit system' for pupils at Key Stage 3;
- refined and altered our achievement monitoring arrangements for Years 7 to 9;
- introduced pupils' portfolios of work for Year 7;

- replaced pupil diaries with a new Pupil Planner to assist in the monitoring of pupils' work and achievement and to assist our communications with parents;
- introduced 'colours' (e.g. in sport) to recognise achievement;
- established rewards for good attendance – both for individuals and for whole forms;
- introduced a system of testing (in reasoning and language skills) in Years 7 to 9 to give further evidence against which we can plot pupil improvement and achievement;
- introduced a new system of achievement monitoring for pupils in Years 10 and 11;
- widened the brief of the examinations officer to include the further development of, and oversight of, assessment and achievement monitoring.

In this school, when the staff received the inspection report, they commented how difficult it was to motivate pupils to succeed. They were aware that it was against the pupils' peer group culture for any pupil (particularly a boy) to work hard, or to be pleased at being praised by staff. The set of strategies outlined above was generated by discussions in a staff working group which acknowledged this difficulty and sought to commit the whole staff to changing the culture for pupils. Strong features of the programme adopted by this school were links between monitoring and action, the involvement of parents and pupils, the introduction of systems that amended or extended those already in existence, and a thorough debate both in a working group and in heads of department meetings.

A report by HMI describes the positive effects of monitoring in another secondary school:

> The criteria for success are made clear to all pupils.
> At Key Stage 3 they know the levels of attainment they have reached, and how they have reached them.
> They know the levels they might aspire to, and what they would have to do to achieve them.
> Before they tackle any assignment they know the criteria by which success will be measured, which attainment targets are being aimed at and the quality of answer required.
> Every decision about the concept and format of the record of achievement is discussed with pupils.
> Improvements in attitudes and motivation have resulted from the opportunity for all pupils to discuss their progress at the end of Year 9.
>
> (OFSTED, 1994)

The practice of talking with individual pupils about the standards they are presently achieving, with a view to helping them to make better progress, is common in many schools. It exemplifies all the best and most useful features of monitoring. It relies on an accurate information base, which is agreed to be relevant by both the person monitoring and the person monitored. It uses targets in a meaningful way. Its principal aim is improvement, and the collection of information takes second place to support and action.

Monitoring the work of individual teachers

It is sometimes hard to interpret the use of the word 'monitor' when it is applied to teaching. Teaching is, of course, one of the principal maintenance activities of a school, as well as being an area for innovation and development. To some extent, therefore, monitoring teaching forms part of monitoring the maintenance activities of a school. In Chapter 2 it was suggested, for instance, that 'routine activities about which there has been agreement among teachers, such as the setting and marking of homework, or the amount of time given to reading in primary classes, can be monitored'. To this limited extent it is possible to envisage 'monitoring' procedures as providing a basic check that agreed policies are being followed.

However the word 'monitor' is currently applied to teaching in a broader sense. In the spring and summer of 1995 groups of primary headteachers were asked how they could best contribute to improving teaching quality, and each group identified 'monitoring of individual teachers at work in their classroom' as a key role for the headteacher. The report of this consultation states:

> Headteachers need to know what is going on in their schools. They need to help staff evaluate the effectiveness of their own teaching. It is only through monitoring, of course, that the head can determine the different support individual teachers might need and the particular contribution each might make to raising teaching standards in the school as a whole.
>
> (OFSTED, 1995d)

In this extract 'monitoring' is used to mean more than a process of information gathering (finding out), and is linked to a deeper and more sustained process of judging quality (normally called evaluation), which involves development and improvement based on reflection and shared discussion.

Many would prefer to use the word evaluation consistently to describe the most effective way of reviewing what happens in classrooms, because this implies that the process should provide information about quality and effectiveness, and focus on the learning as much as on teaching. The OFSTED *Framework* uses both the word 'monitor' and the word 'evaluate' to describe quality assurance processes applied to teaching. In the section of the inspection report dealing with 'leadership and management' judgements are to be made on the extent to which 'teaching and curriculum development are monitored and supported'. In guidance notes the criterion is rephrased as 'Are teaching and curriculum development monitored, evaluated and supported?' There is no doubt about the intention, though. Inspectors, and schools, are reminded that a test of effective leadership and management is the commitment to monitoring and evaluating teaching and the curriculum, and to taking action to sustain and improve their quality. Moreover, finding out about the quality of provision should lead to specific intervention. At subject level the inspection team will investigate whether such interventions have led to improved learning and success for pupils.

To clarify the intention behind the use of different words, these questions need to be asked, and answered, about any review of what happens in classrooms:

- is it mainly about finding out and checking up on people?
- what is to be done with the findings?
- how far are teachers involved in setting the criteria for observation?
- will they get feedback?
- how will interventions and changes be selected, and sustained?

Figure 7 provides a list of questions that should be used by those negotiating classroom observation as part of a monitoring process. There are no right answers; the use of the sheet is intended to contextualise any monitoring activity so that all involved are clear. In some schools which have introduced a new monitoring process there has been insufficient clarity of purpose shared by the observer and the observed, which has minimised the effectiveness of the procedure.

Figure 7 **Negotiating classroom observation (1)**
Before, during and after

Checklist for those observing teachers and support assistants at work in the classroom

Have you any time for a preliminary discussion about the class or the subject being taught?

Is there any prior information you would like the teacher or assistant to let you have?

Will you let them know exactly when you will visit?

How long will you stay? Do they know?

What are you looking at (focus)?

What will you record?

What criteria will you use for recording? Do those being observed know?

Will you show them your notes?

To whom will you report?

If there is a written report can the teacher or assistant see it?

Can they amend it?

What feedback will you give to them? When? Where?
What do you expect them to get from the feedback session?
What do you expect to get from the feedback session?

The quality of teaching is one of the most fundamental aspects for a school to consider as it sets up or extends its self-review procedures. It must be treated very sensitively both because of the major contribution teaching makes to school improvement, and because of the potential impact that new methods of review have on relationships between colleagues and on teachers' confidence. Chapter 6 includes a more extensive discussion of how to introduce observation of classroom practices in a way that can lead to individual reflection on the processes of teaching and learning. A set of questions for those being observed, complementary to those in Figure 7, can be found in Figure 11 on page 139.

Monitoring progress on school plans

Headteachers and governing bodies need to know what is happening in regard to their development plans. An annual review of the previous year's plan, as a preliminary to writing the next one, takes place in many schools. Someone has to collect evidence for such a review, and in larger secondary schools this is often delegated to a deputy headteacher. In smaller secondary, special and primary schools evidence may be collected through meetings between the headteacher and subject co-ordinators. When the time comes for the annual review it can sometimes seem as though there has been no time to implement the plan properly, and the difficulties that have arisen during the year are shown up. This indicates that an annual review is too infrequent for some initiatives, and does not provide the necessary opportunity to revise plans and reallocate resources in time to make a difference. More frequent monitoring may be needed, and should be written into the plan.

Most schools that have taken on an exercise of this type will agree, however, that a review against previously set targets provides a valuable opportunity for taking stock, and for changing direction or the way of working if needed. For instance, one deputy headteacher undertaking such a review found a great variation in the ways different departments had responded to a request to provide examples of the use of differentiated material in teaching. In view of this the school identified the need for in-service training for the whole staff, and for more precise guidelines to subject co-ordinators.

The experience of many schools has been that it is hard to find time to complete a review exercise effectively, and that better planning in advance could improve its usefulness.

The effectiveness of a review of the implementation of development plans, and action plans, depends on

- the clarity of the tasks and targets in the original plan;
- the timing of the collection of evidence for monitoring;
- what is done with the monitoring report;
- the power to take action to amend plans, or to support individuals.

Ideally plans for development should specify clear objectives. This can be done only if the school is clear about the outcome that it is hoping to achieve from actions described in the plan. There should be some statements in school development plans, and action plans, that are sufficiently precise to enable the progress of activity to be monitored efficiently.

Concepts in practice

A practical way of linking these concepts into a monitoring framework is set out in School Planning Sheet 2 on page 202. The purpose of setting up reporting arrangements to monitor action is to prevent problems occurring, or at least to deal with them soon after they become apparent, and to provide both pressure and support to ensure that action is sustained. School Planning Sheet 2 can be used as a supplementary record of action planning for a selected priority.

The school objective is written at the top of the page. The strategy and action steps are summarised in the next section of the report. To complete the section on 'headings for reporting' the school needs to take account of what is manageable, what is practically possible, and what will ensure that things get done. The reports implied by the headings can be brief, and may be informal, though it is often good practice to write something down as well as reporting orally. The sequence of action will imply that reports are made at different times to different groups of people. The reporting schedule described in the last section should be widely known in the school, and governors should be aware of where they will be involved (through an overview such as that provided by School Planning Sheet 1 on page 200).

It is important that this process should not add an unnecessary level of bureaucracy to the demanding tasks of those responsible for action. The planning sheet itself is merely a brief note of agreed and intended practice. Reporting can be fitted into regular meetings, for instance of year groups, or between deputy headteacher and subject co-ordinator.

Maintaining the pace of change

Maintaining the impetus for change and development is one of the most difficult tasks for a school. However well a plan is written, and however much members of staff are involved in identifying ways to deal with the objectives identified, the experience is that action may be neglected for a time for more pressing concerns.

For instance, a secondary school was surveyed eight months after an OFSTED inspection by a visiting HMI, monitoring the action plan. He asked all those he interviewed: 'how do you know that this is really happening?' Answers were reassuring, because the school was in the process of discovering the benefits of internal reporting to help maintain the pace of change. The deputy head had been given a leading responsibility to meet each head of department and to review progress on their department's action plan. He saw this as a dialogue, to remind heads of departments of their responsibilities, and to help them take on the accountability aspect of their role. The review procedures led to a better understanding of the action required, and of the need to monitor.

Monitoring and reporting are valuable activities in their own right and can also lead to changes in the work going on. As a result of the information obtained through monitoring it sometimes becomes clear that something needs to be done differently. In Figure 8, adapted from Figure 1, shown on page 20, the smaller circle shows how feedback from monitoring can lead to change in planned actions.

Figure 8 **A planned approach to improvement (2)**

Some of the changes can be:
- change the timescale;
- change the person responsible, or support them more strongly;
- increase (or reduce) the number of people involved;
- allocate more resources, e.g. find more time for one or more individuals;

- identify a provider of suitable training for staff;
- introduce more clarity into the original plan;
- modify the original objective if it is not sufficiently realistic.

In everyday life, as individuals or within families, people use feedback from the effects of their actions to decide, often unconsciously, whether to continue with them or to modify them. Monitoring provides the same sort of feedback, in a more formal way, for an organisation or group of people. Although there will inevitably be a slower response to the feeding back of information than there is for one individual working on their own, one of the most effective uses of monitoring is to speed up decisions about revising a plan within the year, in order to make action manageable, meaningful and sustainable.

4 School self-evaluation: preparation

· ·

Evaluation goes deeply into the purpose and value of activities. It is a planned process making a systematic study of the quality of what a school is providing.

This chapter sets out some practical considerations for a school setting up a system of self-evaluation to study the quality of its provision. The principles underlying evaluation are discussed and the chapter presents practical methods for collaborative consideration of (i) the purposes of evaluation (ii) ways of selecting a focus and (iii) ways of determining appropriate criteria and indicators for reporting. The planning sheets related to this chapter are intended to be used selectively, with each school considering its own best route to continuing review for improvement.

What is evaluation?

The whole picture of the effectiveness of a school is built up of many pieces of specific knowledge, much of it derived from formal and informal monitoring procedures, such as those described in the last chapter. What is needed is a strategy for linking these together in one coherent view, which provides an illuminating and useful picture of the quality of the work of the school. At times evaluation will require a focus, in depth and specific detail, on selected issues. Each school should adopt its own system, one which suits the people who work there, which is manageable in terms of the resources available, and which eventually proves useful and becomes valued by all involved. This does not happen overnight. Some ideas will be tried and found to be unhelpful; others will be worth modifying and adopting. The suggestions in this chapter and the next are not prescriptive; they are designed for schools to consider, adapt and apply.

The definition of evaluation introduced in Chapter 1 stressed four features which are essential to an understanding of how self-evaluation should be set up in schools.

Evaluation
- is a **systematic** study;
- focuses on the **quality** of provision, and on its impact in terms of outcomes;
- involves the **collection**, **analysis** and **interpretation** of evidence;
- influences **decisions**.

These are all processes that the governors and managers of a school probably engage in, more or less formally, as they determine the spending and allocation of resources year by year. The new stress on formal self-evaluation should not lead to the conclusion that the present processes are irrelevant or inappropriate. Schools should not spend time and energy introducing something apparently new called 'evaluation'. Good advice for a school developing its own strategy is: 'Never adopt a technique using a fashionable name; call it something different so that you have to think it through for yourselves and it fits your situation.' It is as well to couple this with the common-sense advice: 'If it isn't broken, don't mend it.'

For consideration

Evaluation now...

- *How do you know about the quality of what is provided in the school?*

- *How systematically do you review the quality of provision?*
  What standards do you use?
  What evidence is collected?
  How is this analysed and interpreted?
  Where is this reported?
  How does your knowledge of the strengths and weaknesses of the provision influence action?

- *On the basis of your answers above....*
  What is lacking?
  Does this matter?
  Where can improvements be made?

These questions, as do those on pages 69 and 70, enable the headteacher, staff and governors to take stock of the procedures they use at present. In this way a school can look at the key processes described above, and decide if the present application of these processes in the school requires more formalisation, better timetabling, better resourcing or the development of skills for those involved. The next three sections of this chapter provide a framework for considering what evaluation needs to be undertaken more formally, whatever name the school decides to give it. In Chapter 5 there is more detail about the practice in school, with a framework for implementing evaluation.

The six-point framework used in this chapter and the next is based on the acronym **AFFORD**, to remind those planning evaluation of the key questions that should be ans-wered in the school. The acronym also serves as a reminder that evaluation itself has to be viewed critically in terms of the resources it uses. Can the school **afford** to evaluate, or, equally significantly, can it **afford** not to do so?

The six questions of the framework are:

Aims   Why evaluate?
Focus   What should be evaluated?
Features   How should quality be judged?
Organisation How should evidence be collected and analysed?
Reporting   To whom should reports be made, and when?
Decisions   What will be done with the information?

Aims: why evaluate?

What is the evaluation for? What is the principal purpose it is intended to serve? The answers to these questions must have something to do with maintaining and improving the standards in the school. But there will be different specific answers from different individuals, who are at different stages in their response to the introduction of formalised review procedures, with different perceptions of their power and influence, and with different concerns about the work of the school.

Some examples of different situations calling for evaluation are set out below:

> A secondary school had changed the allocation of staffing to ensure that there could be small groups for English and mathematics in Year 7. After one year they wanted to find out whether this shift in the allocation of staffing resources had been a good decision.

> A primary school had falling numbers, and was aware of its poor reputation locally for discipline and academic success. A new headteacher and new chair of governors wanted to find out more objectively what were the causes, and to identify what they could do to improve.

A secondary modern foreign languages department had a record of less success at GCSE than any other department. This was recognised by both the head-teacher, the governors and the members of the department. They agreed that a thorough evaluation of the work of the department, undertaken internally, was more likely to lead to action for change than an external inspection.

A special school, which had recently been reorganised to provide education for pupils with a wider range of special educational needs, wished to involve parents and governors in planning for the future, based on a thorough understanding of the school's present successes.

From these examples it can be seen that there is a variety of reasons, particular to each school's circumstances, that could lead to setting up self-evaluation processes. Some processes will be designed to review the success of a specific innovation, against criteria which should have been set when the innovation was first proposed and funded. The main purpose of this sort of review will be to answer the question 'should we continue to allocate resources in this way?' Others will have action for improvement firmly at the top of their list for reasons for evaluation. Their principal question will be 'what can we do to put this right?' Other schools may be looking for a whole school review that will give answers to the general questions 'what are our strengths, and where should resources and action be directed to the greatest effect?'

Generally schools will need to select a specific focus, because they will recognise the limits of their resources. They will try to find the most appropriate focus for a detailed study, something which is likely to lead to action for change. The process of identifying a productive focus for evaluation is discussed in the next section of this chapter. One risk in self-evaluation that has already been commented on is that the focus and action are not sufficiently strongly linked to teaching and learning, so that the review fails to bring about real change. While this risk must be consciously guarded against it is perhaps less likely now that schools are experiencing a strong pressure to be externally accountable, and are also aware of an emphasis on outcomes, as well as processes, under the OFSTED *Framework* for external inspection.

One of the goals of school evaluation must be personal development for those who work there: 'self-confrontation for self-improvement'. Ownership of the exercise at whole-school level is most important, and staff development is likely to be a crucial, intended, by-product. The first phase of any review will be an experience from which people learn together, and may generate indirect benefits through shared experiences, improved teamwork and confidence. The aims for a first attempt at school self-evaluation should include developing an understanding of evaluation and strengthening of teamwork, as well as improving the quality of teaching and learning in the school. In the second and subsequent phases the school can expect to achieve greater rigour in its evaluation methods, and a greater capability to cope with external pressures and accountability.

Focus: what should be evaluated?

What aspects of school life, of teaching and of learning are to be evaluated? Some of the examples presented earlier in this chapter provide their own answers to the questions above. The need for evaluation may be identified through any of the management processes of a school, and from evidence provided through the monitoring and reflection procedures described in Chapters 3 and 6 of this book. When the focus is easily identified the school can move on to the stage of identifying specific features, indicators and standards, a stage which is discussed in the next section.

If the focus is not easy to select then different methods for developing an overview of the school's work can be used. Two methods are described in the following sections. They can be used to identify possible focuses for more detailed evaluation.

Using a checklist derived from research

The DFE (1995a) advice to governors summarises the characteristics of effective schools, as determined by extensive international research and national school inspection. There are eleven characteristics which can form the basis for a subjective review of the school, perhaps as a starting point for developing better understanding between groups of people (governors, teaching and support staff, for instance). Each of the eleven characteristics has a set of associated questions. In small, preferably mixed, groups staff and governors can begin to answer these questions. This sort of overview, although based on perceptions rather than hard evidence, can serve several purposes by highlighting common areas of concern, sharing an awareness of outside constraints, looking at the values and priorities of different individuals and ultimately identifying areas that need closer attention.

Characteristics of effective schools

1   Professional leadership

a   In what ways does the headteacher communicate a sense of purpose?

b   How does she or he know what goes on in classrooms, and provide support for teachers?

c   How do staff have opportunities to show leadership?

d   In what ways are they involved in decision making?

2   Shared vision and goals

a   To what extent do staff work together with a common sense of purpose?

b   Do they have clear targets?

3   A learning environment

a   Is there an attractive working environment?

b   How does the school provide a climate in which pupils are able to learn?

c   Are the majority of pupils willing to learn?

d   Is the atmosphere for learning orderly?

4   Concentration on teaching and learning

a   In what ways does the school convey a sense of the importance of learning and achievement?

5   Explicit high expectations

a   How does the school communicate its expectations to pupils?

b   How does it set targets for pupils' achievements?

c   How does it ensure that lessons are challenging for all pupils?

6   Positive reinforcement

a   Is discipline perceived to be clear and fair?

b   How do pupils know how well they are doing in their work?

c   How is good work recognised?

7 Monitoring progress

a   What procedures are used to monitor pupils' progress?

b   What monitoring procedures are used for the work of the school as a whole?

8 Pupils' rights and responsibilities

a   How does the school promote pupils' self-esteem?

b   How are they encouraged to take responsibility for their own learning and behaviour?

9 Purposeful teaching

a   Are lessons efficiently organised?

b   Do lessons have a clear sense of purpose?

c   Do lessons take account of the different ways that pupils learn?

d   How does the school ensure that teaching is of consistently high quality?

10 A learning organisation

a   How are adults who work in the school supported in their own learning?

b   How are the needs for staff training and development identified?

c   Are staff development activities valued and effective?

11 Home–school partnership

a   How are relations between home and school fostered?

b   To what extent do parents get actively involved in their children's work and in the life of the school?

The OFSTED inspection *Framework* (1995b) provides a more extensive checklist of questions, which inspectors use to summarise a whole school profile (see Appendix 1 on page 185). This is appropriate for a similar exercise with teaching staff. A 22-question checklist based on the OFSTED subject profile summary (see Appendix 2 on page 190) could be used with a group of people whose main concern is the teaching of a specific subject.

In any approach based on an externally generated checklist it is important to acknowledge, and to work with, the difficulty and frustration people will have in attempting to answer some of the questions. There will be differences of opinion: some will say 'how can we possibly know?' and some will say that the answers are different in different departments and for different teachers. Any of these responses is valid and useful. The exercise is only of value at school level in terms of what it leads to next. In the context of the stages of evaluation the discussion should be used to decide on a focus to be looked at more systematically, ultimately to determine more precisely and objectively how well the school is doing.

Working collaboratively with different interest groups

A different approach was taken by a research team from the University of Strathclyde (MacBeath et al., 1996), asked by the National Union of Teachers (NUT) to develop a self-evaluation framework for schools. The team piloted an approach that involved parents, pupils, teaching and non-teaching staff in generating lists of what was important for them about a school. The team's aim was to create a framework based on the indicators of effectiveness defined by different interest groups. Although the project was aimed at identifying criteria and, ultimately, instruments for collecting evidence, it also crucially recognised the need for the framework for self-evaluation to be workable and user-friendly.

The team reported the basis of their approach with English and Welsh schools:

> With all groups in all the schools, the same approaches were used – firstly an invitation to list individually their own five key factors of an effective school (done as a brainstorming exercise where there were language or writing difficulties). Secondly, a card sort exercise was used with 23 criteria drawn from OFSTED guidelines for school inspection plus two blanks for people to add their own. Small groups were asked to agree on the five

most important criteria for them and then to do the same with the three criteria which they considered to be least important. With very young pupils we used variations of these approaches, for example asking them to draw the things they liked best about schools and their teachers, following this up with questioning and discussion.

(Boyd, MacBeath and Rand, 1995)

This approach acknowledges that different interest groups may have different values and expectations. Not surprisingly, the team found that perceptions of good schools offered by parents, pupils and teachers did not differ greatly from those found by researchers into school effectiveness. Although there was a strong consensus across all schools on the key elements of the good school, there were also significant differences from group to group and from school to school.

Working in this way provides a sense of what is really important for those with the greatest concerns about an individual school. It can therefore provide a basis for identifying a focus. It also takes the school closer to generating meaningful school-based criteria for making judgements. The language used in phrases contributed by pupils ('Miss A treats you like a real human being, she listens, she never talks down to you or fobs you off') or parents ('the school has a buzz in its atmosphere when you go in') or teachers ('issues are dealt with promptly and not allowed to fester') breathes life into the dry statements of, for instance, the OFSTED checklists.

The drawback is the number of statements such an approach can generate. The Scottish team records being left with 1,743 individual indicators, which it was able to group into clusters. It is unlikely that an individual school will have the resources to process and sort out such a wealth of information, however valuable it is. The 'indicator clusters' defined as a result of the research described above have much in common with the 'school effectiveness' headings that the DFE (1995a) recommends to governors. However, knowing how they have been derived, some schools may prefer to work from the list from the NUT/Strathclyde project, and involve parents, pupils and teachers as much as they can afford to.

The team derived these 10 indicator clusters:
- School climate
- Relationships
- Classroom climate
- Support for learning
- Support for teaching

- Time and resources
- Organisation and communication
- Equity
- Recognition of achievement
- Home school links

(MacBeath et al., 1996: p 28)

The project team conclude that, although a common framework for self-evaluation by schools can usefully be built up, it is essential that it is flexible enough to allow modification by individual schools to meet their own particular purpose and a local context. At the stage of choosing a focus, and the next stage of selecting features (criteria), a school has to find practical and cost-effective ways of using that flexibility. Sometimes, for some schools, externally prepared checklists and evaluation criteria will seem appropriate. At other times an investment in investigating and creating something unique to the school will be worthwhile.

Practical considerations

One important consideration in selecting a focus, by whatever means, is not to overstretch the resources a school has to gather and assimilate information. However important it is to review an area of the school's work a prudent judgement has to be made about what the school can find time for, and what is likely to be effective. There should be a limited number of evaluation strategies at any one time. Teachers, parents and governors are more likely to see the value of something that is carried through to action with beneficial changes. A school should make a decision about its priorities for evaluation, and then reduce the list to not more than one or two focus areas in a year (see School Planning Sheets 1 and 6 on pages 200, 206 and 208).

Features: how should quality be judged?

The word 'features' is used here to refer to the standards that the school would expect to achieve in the chosen focus area. It stands for the 'criteria' or the 'performance indicators' that seem most appropriate to use in judging the quality of an aspect of the school's work. In Chapter 3 the idea of 'report headings' for monitoring activities was introduced. Some of these report headings include indicators which are quantifiable (for example, the frequency of reading assessment for each pupil in School Planning Sheet 2 on page 202. Report headings are a practical substitute for criteria, provided that they derive from a collective decision about the high standards aimed for.

The task of identifying features for evaluation, whether it be for an action plan, for elements of the development plan or for a whole school review, is often presented as simpler than it seems to be in school. As one critic commented: 'To ask schools to produce clear criteria against which to judge their effectiveness is to set a complex task under the guise of apparent simplicity.' The work of the Strathclyde team, described in the last section, shows how valuable such an attempt can be, especially if not only teachers are involved in setting the criteria. Useful, meaningful and manageable criteria can be found if the school has a method for the task. Features selected to be used in evaluation should be **few** in number, **specific**, **clearly expressed**, **relevant** to the focus and **capable of being investigated**. Wherever possible they should include **measures** of pupils' achievement. When appropriate significant features have been selected and some evidence has been gathered, judgements can be made about the worth and effectiveness of the school's decisions and provision.

Alternative methods for generating lists of features

Method 1 – Future images

Once a focus has been selected groups of people are asked to complete School Planning Sheet 3 (shown on page 203), first as individuals, then collectively. The focus under consideration is stated at the top of the page. In completing the section headed the 'The Future' individuals are asked to express their hopes, using their creativity and imagination. Each person in the group can contribute ideas, with as much informality as possible. In describing the ideal state people should be encouraged to make mental pictures. For instance, if pupils had more 'responsibility for their own learning', what would be happening in practice? If pupils 'used information technology resources more efficiently', where would this be seen, what would they experience, and what would be the results in terms of capability? For each group a record can be made of some of the key indicators suggested by the 'image' of the future.

The practical outcome of this imaginative process is that the different descriptions can be collected together, summarised (as shown in School Planning Sheet 4 on page 204) and used to derive a short list of observable features of the ideal state of affairs. These may include specific measurable indicators. They act as a guide to those collecting and analysing the evidence, and provide a framework for those presenting, and receiving, the evaluation reports.

Method 2 – Generating a list
An alternative approach involves generating a list of indicators, which relate to the standards expected, from a shared understanding of the focus. This method can be used

to explore what a selected focus means to people in the school. A general statement of school effectiveness can be interpreted locally by asking supplementary questions.

Suppose the focus selected is 'An environment that supports learning'. This focus can be found in several lists as a good thing in itself, but its meaning is fairly obscure until it is interpreted in a particular school by those who have a close connection with it.

In order to expand on the focus
- teachers can be asked 'How would we know that we had an environment that supports learning?'
- pupils can be asked 'What helps you to learn?'
- parents can be asked 'What most helps your child to make progress?'

Some answers like these might be received:
- good behaviour in classrooms;
- parents and pupils have easy access to teachers, who listen to them;
- teachers know how well each child is doing;
- there are adequate and up-to-date books and equipment;
- there is a well cared for space that is safe for challenging activities.

School Planning Sheet 5 on page 205 illustrates another set of questions for expanding a focus into specific, recognisable features.

In each case it is important to check:

- Are the features selected few in number, specific, clearly expressed, relevant to the focus and capable of being investigated?
- Do they include any measures of pupils' achievement?

Figure 9 gives an example of a school moving from a focus to generating an evaluation strategy, one which will enable evidence to be collected and judgements made. The next chapter deals with the practical implementation of such strategies, and with the issue of making sure that they lead to action.

Figure 9 **A school generating an evaluation strategy from a focus question**

Question

Is there a shared sense of teamwork amongst staff?

How would we know?

Quantitative measures

Opportunities for joint staff working in the timetable.

Incidence of shared planning and teaching.

Participation in school committees and working parties.

Qualitative measures

Staff feel their views are valued.

Staff seek out colleagues for support.

Staff feel ownership of policies.

Staff value use of INSET.

How will we go about finding out?

Survey of uses of staff time.

Analysis of school documentation, e.g. minutes, timetable.

Staff feedback forms, e.g. evaluation of INSET.

Peer observation and interview.

(OFSTED, 1994)

5 School self-evaluation: implementation

• •

Evaluation may use a range of methods for collecting evidence. In evaluation information is analysed and interpreted, and judgements made and reported. Evaluation should have an effect on future decisions and action.

The previous chapter dealt with the first three topics signalled by the acronym AFFORD: Aims, Focus and Features. In this chapter Organisation, Reporting and Decisions are discussed. The latter stages of an evaluation process involve the collection of evidence, analysis and interpretation, formation of judgements and reporting of those judgements in a way that ensures that effective action can be taken. As well as discussing these steps, this chapter indicates some changes that may be required within a school, as it devises its own systems.

Organisation and methods: how should evidence be collected and analysed?

The example set out in Figure 9 at the end of the last chapter shows how the identification of features of the focus leads on to consideration of the organisation of the evaluation and the methods to be used to collect and use evidence.

Key questions as this stage begins are:

- what evidence is to be gathered and by what means?
- who will undertake collection, analysis and reporting?
- what resources will be available?
- when will evaluation take place?
- what will it cost?

A variety of methods can be chosen, some of them using people within the school in new roles, and in new combinations, and some involving outsiders. Figure 10 sets out a range of possible alternatives, and is intended as a prompt sheet for the best way to organise an evaluation. Innovative and productive new combinations can be generated by considering possible selections of items from each column.

Once the school has reached the stage of planning organisation of the evaluation, the focus will have been selected. The first column lists some possible focuses. The second, third and fourth columns provide suggestions about varied approaches to evaluation. As an illustration of the use of the prompt sheet assume that the school has selected 'positive discipline' as its focus. Evidence could, for example, be collected by a deputy headteacher by means of a survey of

Figure 10 **Organisation of evaluation**

Evidence about	Collected by	By means of	Analysed by	Reported to	Resourced from
Standards	Head	Tracking pupils	Coordinator	Whole staff	Management duties
Teaching	Deputy	Questionnaires	Deputy	Governors	Directed time
Curriculum	Coordinator	Observation	Head	Parents	GEST funding
Discipline	Outsider	Observation and reflection	Group of teachers	Head	Volunteers
Support for staff	Governor	Survey of views			INSET days
Home–school	Teacher	Pupil interviews			Supply cover
Leadership	Pupils	Group discussion			
Relationships	School review team	Peer evaluation			
Resources					

staff, for return to a working group who would analyse the findings and ultimately report back to the whole staff. For this exercise the resource would be the management time of the deputy, some administrative support, and directed time for the working group and the staff meeting.

Another illustration is provided by a special school which needed to evaluate the effectiveness of the work that had gone into a project for teaching autistic children. Evidence was collected by the headteacher, by means of observation and talking with parents. She analysed the evidence with the co-ordinator of the project, and they reported to the governing body. The evaluation work formed part of the responsibilities of both headteacher and co-ordinator. If they had wished to involve other teachers, they would have taken up the option of using some supply cover.

Figure 10 suggests that evidence can be collected by the headteacher, a deputy, a co-ordinator, an outsider, a governor, teachers, pupils, a specially constituted school review team – any combination of these. To gather evidence any of the following methods can be used: tracking pupils, questionnaires, focused observation, reflection, survey of views, interviews with pupils or parents, peer evaluation. Once findings have been gathered they must be analysed and judgements formed. This can be the responsibility of, for instance, a co-ordinator, a deputy, the headteacher or a group of teachers.

In each of the illustrations above it is clear that the link between the identification of criteria and the collection and analysis of evidence is an important one, and it is in this area that many teachers will feel that they need support and advice. For instance, it may be advisable to agree a level of confidentiality in evidence gathering, preserving anonymity and not revealing the contributions of individuals outside an agreed group of people. The school should consider how to build on the present skills and experience of its own staff, and also how to use the support of LEA advisers and other consultants, as well as links with higher education (maybe through teachers attending part-time award-bearing courses). Some of these ideas for support are explored in more depth in Chapter 7.

Reporting:
to whom should a report be made, and when?

Questions need to be asked about what is to be done with the findings from the evaluation, once evidence has been collected and analysed, and judgements made. To whom will the findings be made available, and when? What will be the extent of openness or confidentiality? The answers to these questions will depend on the purpose of the evaluation exercise and, in particular, on how it is expected to lead to action.

Managing a realistic timetable for both monitoring and evaluation is important. School Planning Sheet 1 (shown on page 200) was introduced in Chapter 3 as a way of placing on record an overview of the monitoring and evaluation that is going on in a school, grouped under key headings. This overview is an opportunity to ensure that the reporting arrangements are practical, that the governing body is fully aware, and that the school has not engaged in too many data-gathering exercises at one time.

School Planning Sheet 6 is a timetable for evaluation, reporting and action. Sheets 6P and 6S (pages 206 and 208) are primary and secondary school examples of the use of this sheet, showing more detailed planning for evaluation, and about how reporting may be linked to planning and action. Decisions about appropriate levels of reporting should relate not only to how the evidence has been gathered, but also to what action is expected as a result of the report. For example, the issue of reviewing teaching quality on sheet 6S shows how a secondary school chooses to report on this through a deputy headteacher, and that this report is intended to lead to action planning at department level, and to a later report to governors, incorporating the findings from the evaluation and the planned action. On Sheet 6P, a primary school sets out a timetable for evaluating a scheme to involve parents with children's reading. Both the collection of evidence and the reporting stages involve the parents themselves.

One important purpose of a summary sheet of this type is to ensure that a school takes account of what can practically be afforded. An overview is essential in order to plan for a limited number of evaluation programmes at any one time. It is suggested that a school takes on a maximum of two (possibly three for a large secondary school) evaluation exercises in an academic year.

Illustrations of timetables for reporting

A primary school evaluating parental involvement in reading (from 6P):
> In the spring and summer terms the school establishes its evaluation criteria, collects and analyses the evidence. The headteacher is able to report the findings to the whole staff at the end of the summer term, to hear their reactions and suggestions, and to incorporate these in a report to governors and parents during the autumn term. Later in the autumn the staff can make

their proposals for action, to improve the effectiveness of what has been evaluated. While some of these proposals may have been put into effect from September, because of the early consideration of the findings by the teachers in June, others will have implications for further resourcing (books, time) and can be passed on to the governors, from the staff, in order to be incorporated in the planning round for the next year's budget allocation.

This example highlights the fact that teachers, governors and parents will need to know different things, in different levels of detail. Those presenting reports need to bear this in mind, and to summarise findings as appropriate. The levels of confidentiality agreed when the evidence is gathered should be scrupulously observed.

A secondary school evaluating its working environment (from 6S):

The focus of the 'working environment' in a secondary school is examined using the criteria determined by a staff working group meeting during the latter part of the summer term. In the following autumn term pupils from all year groups are involved in collecting information, by means of a survey. The results are analysed by the senior management team in the spring term, in time to report to the governors so that they can make appropriate decisions when they approve the school budget, and so that any improvement work to premises and grounds can be undertaken before the following academic year.

In this example a long time is allowed for the exercise, so that careful planning for reporting at the right level places the governors in a good position to weigh up priorities on the basis of sound information.

Decisions and development: what will be done with the information?

To what use will the evaluation be put? By what process will it feed into decision making and action? The principal purpose of gathering information is to bring about change if it is needed. Some changes do indeed take place informally, as a consequence of people reflecting on and discussing what has been found out as part of evaluation. However, in a large institution some change has to be planned for, particularly so that it can be resourced. The reporting arrangements illustrated in the previous section should relate to the times of the year when groups of people get together to plan. Year teams and departments, governors' sub-committees, the whole staff, the senior management group – all have cycles of working together and of making decisions. Parents and pupils make their decisions too, about their level of interest in, and support for, what the school can offer. Reporting should be carefully timed so that developments can be planned and decisions made.

In considering action on the basis of evaluation a school should

- recognise that some decisions are made informally;
- relate evaluation to subject, department and school development planning;
- use evaluation to justify allocating further resources where possible;
- relate evaluation to external inspection and advice;
- relate evaluation to the planning of staff development activities;
- use evaluation to create a confident learning organisation.

Changes that may be required in the school

To undertake school self-evaluation, even selectively, implies changes in a school. Successful internal review schemes are realistic about collecting data, and avoid time-consuming processes. They

- enable a wide range of people to be involved (pupils,

- parents, community, support staff);
- gather information for internal use;
- lead to action for improvement in terms that make sense to all those who work in the school.

The school has to ask what needs to change, and how changes will be made, in order to make its self-review processes effective. Answers will be different for different schools.

For consideration

How can

- people be motivated to become involved?
- evaluation skills be developed for all staff?
- sufficient time be found for evaluation?
- the school gain experience in planning change, and in managing commitment and time?
- improvements be made to the rigour and objectivity of evaluation?
- the effort make a real difference to pupils' learning?

Each school should consider and make decisions about the changes needed to adopt and use its own preferred systems, prompted by the headings below.

Formality

How formal should school self-evaluation be? Can it be introduced gradually, building on existing procedures? What names should be given to new activities?

Timing

A choice of timing, for introduction as well as for reporting, which takes account of the institution's specific needs, conditions and culture with regard to development, can avoid a sense of pointless overload.

Resourcing

Time is the most important resource. It has to be acknowledged that doing something new means doing less of something else. What might be lost? What new resources can be introduced?

Skill development

All aspects of institutional evaluation demand that those involved learn new skills, and apply those that they already have in different ways. Some evaluation skills are learned collaboratively in the school, but the support of outsiders, whether as advisers, researchers or trainers, may be needed. This aspect of development is dealt with in more detail in the next chapter.

In the collaborative model recommended throughout this book teachers and others specifically need the skills and commitment to

- identify the subset of questions which need the closest consideration at any given time;
- generate a set of qualitative indicators relating to each of these questions;
- define the methods that will be used to collect evidence about these indicators;
- decide how to move from the evaluative stage to action for change;
- set targets;
- monitor the effects of the action.

A climate of evaluation

New strategies of evaluation will only become accepted if they lead to perceived benefits in people's working lives. Any strategy is unlikely to be sustainable if no improvement ensues. In most schools a self-evaluation approach linked to action will become accepted if pupils are getting something out of it, if on a day-to-day basis teachers' conditions of work are improved, and if all can see a measurable increase in success for pupils. After introducing and trying out new systems, a school should subject them to critical scrutiny.

Has it been worth introducing school self-evaluation?

- How much of what we intended to achieve has been done?
- Have we met the deadlines for reports?
- Was the timescale realistic?
- Did we choose the right number of evaluation focuses?
- Were the right criteria chosen?
- Were the judgements made accepted by those most closely involved?
- What changes have they made?
- What impact has evaluation had on the attainment and progress of pupils?
- Have there been any unexpected benefits, and have we acknowledged these?
- Does the degree of improvement justify the time and expenditure on what we have done?

6 Reflecting on teaching and learning

A school which demonstrates confidence in its teachers can create a climate of creativity where each person can contribute new ideas, and new energy, to the development of the school as a whole.

This chapter is about tactics for reflecting on change in the classroom. It acknowledges the feelings of stress in schools, and looks at the effects of support and pressure. By recounting some experiences in individual schools it illustrates different ways of introducing classroom observation and shared reflection in order to improve the quality of teaching. It explores the question of the links, and tensions, between monitoring formally and creating a climate of openness and creativity.

Opening the classroom doors

The challenge for school self-review is to bring about change where it really counts. The rational model that links evaluation and change proposes a cycle (see Figure 1 on page 20). Earlier chapters of this book have shown how a school can plan activities based on this model. As a basis for making real changes, however, this determinist model, which assumes that cause and effect can be predicted, has some limitations. Rational planning must be moderated by feedback, and has to be flexible enough to respond to changed internal or external conditions. Furthermore, the very general model ('monitoring brings about improvement') has to be applied with sensitivity to the particular needs and conditions in any institutional or individual situation. Real change comes about through a process with levels of uncertainty that need to be explored.

> *Scientific certainty*, the certainty grounded in proven principles of generalised applicability, is being replaced by *situated certainty*; the certainty that teachers and others can collectively glean from their shared practical knowledge of their immediate context and the problems it presents. This school-based search for missions, visions and continuous improvement gives much needed weight to the validity of practitioner knowledge and to the needs and demands of each particular context within which these practitioners work.
>
> (Hargreaves A, 1994: p 59)

The challenge facing many headteachers is how to open the classroom doors, metaphorically and physically, so that it is possible find some 'shared practical knowledge'. These headteachers are trying to create a climate where talking frankly about teaching is acceptable, and enlightening. They often do this by a blend of formal and informal means, at least initially. The four accounts that follow are from head-teachers who have chosen to operate in different ways, each motivated by a need to know what is happening and a desire to help teachers to improve.

Headteachers' accounts

One thing I find strange in schools is the way that people will close doors and cover windows – with dis-plays, for instance. People say it is to stop pupils looking in, but I don't think it is just that. One of the things I wanted to do in my first term as headteacher was get it accepted that I could just walk into any class-room on an informal basis. We've got an OFSTED inspection next year, so I explained that I wanted to get a feel for the ethos of the school – one way of finding evidence that will present the school in a true light to inspectors. At the same time I wanted this to be seen as a way that we could use to share concerns and prob-lems, so that we could find solutions – an opening up of information so it can affect practice.

(Secondary school headteacher)

What I have done was to arrange to spend every half term with a new department. I make sure I see every teacher teaching and teaching in every year. So I have seen every single member of staff teach, and seen teaching within all the year groups. This means that I know what is going on in each department and each year. I am not attempting to monitor the teachers as an appraiser might. Rather, what I am looking at is the way the children are receiving the lesson. I sit with the children.

(Secondary school headteacher:
BEMAS Conference 1995)

When I first came here there was a lack of procedures, strategies, accountability; I had to put into place policies and procedures so that staff knew what was expected of them. We've arrived at a situation where I've now developed a culture where staff with curriculum responsibilities are beginning to feel more confident and take on the responsibility for their curriculum areas and work with other staff in ensuring the policies and schemes of work that should be being worked are in place. At the same time I'm now introducing a system where I go into each class each week and concentrate on that specific class. I see the children's work, I see every child in the class at a specific task whatever the teacher has chosen and at the same time I'm using that non-threatening opportunity, to go round talking to children, looking back on work seeing how they have progressed and so on. Instinctively I pick up how that class is operating, the sort of levels of concentration within the class; the use of helpers; the displays on the walls, and then I give feedback to that member of staff at lunchtimes. I do it on a Monday, so part of Monday lunchtime I spend giving them feedback. I haven't got to the stage yet which I had in my other school where I do a written feedback.

(Primary school headteacher:
BEMAS Conference 1995)

I believe if the head of department is regularly looking at the work in the department and recording what they see on summary sheets which are produced regularly for me then we have got it about right. That plus the regular department meetings, that really is what I expect to see in terms of the head of department role. I would like to see heads of departments spend more time in classrooms and I've said that to them. I would not expect it done to a standard form. In practical terms people tend to keep their own notes and complete the summary sheets later. There is a recognition that the head of department visits classrooms in some departments, but it's not even got started in other departments. I don't think there should be a difficulty about whether they go in to check up, or whether there is seen to be a more developmental aspect – the two are not incompatible. It's how it is presented to departments; 'I must come into your lessons, I've got to', is not a healthy way of introducing it, but at the end of the day if it turned out that there was an inadequate member of staff then that head of department has to have the means to inform me, otherwise it's the head of department who is accountable for those poor results. But there are different ways of doing this which would be appropriate for each department. The bottom line is I can't expect all people to behave the same, but I would expect them to have found ways as professionals to have visited classrooms.

(Secondary school headteacher)

The first headteacher described his introduction of new behaviour (a head visiting classrooms) as a 'trojan mouse'. His first objective was to change the climate. The last headteacher quoted makes it clear that at some time the tensions between accountability and development have to be faced. The skilled leader works in the knowledge of this tension, changing the climate and teachers' expectations by activities that demonstrate the value of shared discussion, and being prepared formally to clarify requirements and responsibilities, as necessary. Sensitivity to the situation seems to mean that in practice people use a judicious blend of formal and informal strategies. Researchers into school improvement have found that real change does not come about without 'internal turbulence' in the school. The last headteacher quoted above was well aware that the process of bringing about the change she wanted would not be smooth and comfortable.

There is increasing agreement, however, that evaluation of classroom practice is a necessary shared activity. There is a widespread expectation that school staff should regularly undertake an internal review exercise, and some choose to use OFSTED guidelines. Each of the various ways that the headteachers quoted above have chosen to 'open the classroom doors' in their schools is a form of monitoring. What their different stories illustrate is the need to select a process that can both prove acceptable now and, ultimately, challenge and change the school's culture – change it towards one of shared reflection on practice.

Changing roles and responsibilities

As a school adopts new methods of self-review, attitudes to personal accountability as well as to personal development will change. There may be formal changes in responsibilities, or changes in expectations and ways of working. Many of these changes affect particularly those in middle management roles, for instance allowance holders, curriculum and key stage co-ordinators in special and primary schools, and heads of department and pastoral team leaders in secondary schools. The Teacher Training Agency (TTA) has recognised this in setting out its targets for continuous in-service training of teachers over the next few years. It asserts (TTA, 1995) that 'good leadership and management at subject level is essential if the quality of teaching and learning is to be systematically and effectively monitored, evaluated and improved' and that training to improve subject teaching in the primary phase should focus on 'subject co-ordinators, who are central to ensuring that all children receive effective specialist teaching'.

In many schools it is external inspection that has brought pressure to bear on middle managers, and for some there have been uncomfortable changes. Heads of department are sometimes reluctant to visit their colleagues' classrooms unless the focus is agreed to be entirely developmental and supportive. However, they recognise that, with the current emphasis on monitoring teaching quality, their visits cannot be completely free of an 'inspectorial' function, and they are often concerned about the use that could be made of their reports on their colleagues. Some feel that this has substantially altered the relationships in their departments:

> I can no longer be the friend, without the big stick. It could well be that I have to go to people and say I'm sorry but you're just not good enough, and I do feel that that is a role which I haven't had before. People are more wary now of me and what I think, and where my thoughts go, to the head, to OFSTED, to HMI… There is not that friendship, that camaraderie. It seems to me that head of department will gradually be isolated from the troops.
>
> (Head of department, secondary school)

There are some echoes here of the apprehensions around the introduction of appraisal into schools. The process of appraisal is expected to improve teaching, and learning. Whereas inspection and the inspectorial role may be associated with the 'big stick', conversely, in many schools appraisal has often been introduced so gently, with kid gloves, that it has had little effect on the improvement of teaching and learning. The tensions between accountability and development were thoroughly discussed throughout the whole run-up to appraisal of teachers, with the National Steering Group's report stressing that appraisal should be

- formative not summative;
- negotiated;
- concerned with future rather than past performance;
- matched to criteria for development;
- related to explicit staff development strategies;

and that, as a process, it should

- analyse performance rather than judge it;
- produce personal targets for growth;
- recognise the significance of organisational goals as well as the need for personal development.

The appraisal schemes developed nationally and locally for teachers have been careful explicitly to separate 'evaluation' and 'development', because of the perception that these goals could be in conflict. It appears now that such a clear separation cannot be preserved in the monitoring responsibilities of heads of department. Realistically the headteacher quoted above saying 'I don't think there should be a difficulty about whether they go in to check up, or whether there is seen to be a more developmental aspect – the two are not incompatible' recognised that the problem has to be surmounted in practice.

One way of being open about the tensions is to recognise that there are questions that teachers have a right to ask about classroom visits. It may not seem appropriate to deal with these formally on every occasion in every school, but it is helpful for both the visitor and the visited to be aware that they could be asked, and should be answered. The questions in Figure 11 mirror those in Figure 7 on page 85.

Figure 11 **Negotiating classroom observation (2)**

Questions that teachers and classroom assistants may wish to ask about any observer in the classroom.

Whenever anyone is observing you teach you should be able first to check on the answers to these questions.

Have you any time for a preliminary discussion about the class or the subject being taught?

Is there any prior information you would like the observer to have?

Do you know when the observer will visit?

How long will she/he stay?

What are they looking at (focus)?

What will they record?

What criteria will they use for recording?

Will you be able to see their notes?

To whom will they report?

Can you see their report?

Can you amend it?

What feedback will they give you? When? Where?

What do you expect to get from the feedback session?

In school self-evaluation schemes the expectation is that heads of department, and those with curriculum responsibilities in primary and special schools, know about the quality of teaching, and that they gain this knowledge through first-hand observation that is more extensive than that which may take place under an appraisal scheme. Where this implies a change in practice for individuals, and teams, it is healthy to discuss some of the questions above.

Expectations of curriculum leaders

Accountability without development is sterile. Finding out about the quality of teaching should lead to some specific change, perhaps to some specific intervention. At subject level such interventions should lead to improved learning and success for pupils.

One description of key functions of a curriculum leader provides a positive view of what can be achieved through monitoring and sharing perceptions of teaching. These functions are:

- motivating staff;
- building morale;
- demonstrating good practice in their own teaching;
- engaging in critical self-evaluation;
- seeking improvement through working with others to share ideas and to learn from experience.

Heads of department and curriculum leaders should be enabled to set time aside for regular discussion with other members of staff, particularly newly qualified and trainee teachers, and should be sensitive to the needs of individual teachers without losing sight of the overall responsibility for the quality of education provided for all pupils in the subject. Areas for improvement in subject teaching can be targeted by teams. Teachers can work effectively in pairs or groups to co-operate in presenting their ideas to colleagues, or to tackle new tasks on behalf of the department as a whole. Ideally those with leadership roles should aim to create a climate where teachers are prepared to acknowledge difficulties, and to seek help readily because they are confident that support is there.

Changes for teams

One teacher talked of the difficulty of sustaining changes in her teaching style, and of the need for the support of other department members:

> It doesn't take a lot of time, a lot of effort, to say, 'Right, every lesson I am going to do this.' But I think it's very hard to change the deep-rooted habits of a lifetime as a teacher, and you need something that helps you to do this. Unless I'm doing it, and setting myself a

goal of doing it, then the whole monitoring thing has been a waste of time.

> (Secondary school teacher)

Where departments agree to focus together on a specific change in teaching style there is the potential for keeping motivation and commitment high:

> We found it was more successful if the department agreed what was the focus of the observation rather than it being on the teacher. For example, if our aim was to introduce this technique or staff resource or new scheme of work, we'd ask how much have we achieved with that. Can we look and see if by doing that we have actually achieved what we hoped to achieve, or is it irrelevant – has it not changed anything – or has it changed in some places and not in others? We could then feed back in departmental discussions that would come to conclusions.
>
> (Deputy headteacher, Secondary school)

One of the primary schools visited by the research teams looking at effective schools in disadvantaged areas on behalf of the National Commission on Education (1996) had developed several strategies to allow curriculum co-ordinators to influence the quality of their colleagues' teaching. Each Monday morning the headteacher spends two hours in a different class, observing the teacher and talking to the children about their work. She follows this up with a discussion with the teacher. In addition every teacher has a period of release time each week which they can use for planning. The curriculum co-ordinators get some time to work with their colleagues in the classroom, and also have one and a half days to attend subject-specific INSET. Finding time, as well as creating a climate, for curriculum leaders in primary and special schools to undertake their responsibilities is a very difficult issue in many schools, and can best be tackled by setting priorities for curriculum review and improvement, and targeting resources within a term or a year.

Involving support staff

As schools develop new procedures it is important to involve all staff, support staff as well as teachers. One head-teacher stressed the importance of this in her school:

> Some of my best staff are non-teaching staff. Some of my teachers used to teach in schools where non-teaching staff were not allowed in staff rooms. They were not considered to be an equal part of the school and yet you cannot move a school forward without everybody pulling together. This view of everybody going in

the same direction and planning the future together is so important. When we have meetings, everybody comes. The governors come, teachers' aides, nursery nurses, secretarial staff, they are all there – we have done a lot of working together, and also lots of breaking down into smaller groups. Every group has a cross-section of the school population in it working on different aspects and then bringing it back to talk about to everybody else and that has worked extremely well. One of the things I am doing at the moment is Investors in People. You have to include everybody, as it's fatal to forget. We use GNVQs. We are looking at training our staff properly as far as Investors in People is concerned and we have ten non-teaching staff (mid-day supervisors, non-teaching assistants and teachers' aides) who are working on GNVQs related to the work that they do. We have managed to get funding to pay for it. We are also offering placements to other people too.

(Primary school headteacher:
BEMAS Conference 1995)

Tactics for observation and reflection

Some tactics for using classroom observation to improve teaching are implied in the accounts of experiences of schools reported in the last two sections. These accounts show the need for a creative balance between informality and formality, between whole-school 'top-down' initiatives and the encouragement of specific new ways of working that may be effective for teams and subgroups.

One way of introducing change at classroom level is through collaborative research in pairs and teams. Teachers can look for shared solutions to problems encountered in the classroom, try out new ideas and feed back to each other on their success. This approach is based on a particular view of the professionalism of teachers: that they should be skilled practitioners, continually reflecting on their practice in terms of ideals and knowledge of local situations, and modifying practice in the light of these reflections, rather than technicians applying teaching programmes devised by others. The traditional 'action research' cycle is action, observation, analysis, evaluation and further planning. Some of the strategies adopted by key stage and departmental teams resemble this approach, and have the strengths of action research – that is, are teacher-centred so that each teacher gains from the group. In order to relate such individually inspired initiatives to targets for raising standards of achievement of pupils, it is argued here that a degree more formality is needed, together with some co-ordination, specific requirements of individuals and support for them at a whole-school level. This is because it is difficult to use 'reflection' effectively. It has to mean more than just thinking; it should imply some re-examination of theories, personal as well as public, and some observation of practice, and analysis of what is seen.

Reflection

Griffiths and Tann (1992) propose a useful classification of five levels of reflection which are easily recognisable, and which relate both to immediate reactions and also to increasingly complex and sustained changes in the way an individual teacher works:

Level 1   Reflection-in-action
This is likely to be personal and private. The teacher acts, and reacts almost instinctively. For instance if one child asks for a spelling the response is immediate, but would be different for different teachers.

Level 2   Reflection which 'repairs'
Instant individual monitoring gives rise to a replanning of lesson tactics. A child's response, or question, may give a

teacher new insight about the content and the pupils' understanding of it. There is a brief opportunity to pause for thought, and a quick readjustment.

Level 3 Reflection on action – reviewing

This is likely to be interpersonal and collegial – something the teacher can discuss with others. It is the sort of reflection that often goes on during the journey home, or at the end of the day in the staff room. As a result of this reflection the whole teaching plan may be modified, worksheets abandoned or redrafted, new stimulus material introduced, different tasks set for pupils.

Level 4 Reflection as research

Observation becomes systematic and sharply focused – possibly with a peer partner or an 'expert' colleague. In planning the observation, and in analysing the feedback, the teacher will reflect on why the issue has arisen, decide on a process for gathering evidence, and decide what has worked and what can be done differently.

Level 5 Reflection leading to new personal theories

This is the most challenging level, because it may take a teacher beyond their present expectation of what teaching is about. In this model the teachers evaluate systematically, analyse rigorously, evaluate and develop new theories, before further planning and action. Over a period of months or years, if such activity is sustained, the teachers may themselves develop new views of teaching and challenge accepted theories.

In considering tactics for using classroom observation as a means of improving teaching it is important to value all these levels, as well as noting that observation can occur on a spectrum from the individual to the collective, from the optional to the imposed, with methods that are sometimes more, and sometimes less, under the control of the observed. Ted Wragg (1994) writes that 'skilfully handled, classroom observation can benefit both the observer and the person observed, serving to inform and enhance the professional skill of both people'. His book, based on this belief, provides many practical illustrations of the variety of methods of recording and analysis that can be used under different circumstances. It is an important resource, as well as a useful reminder that methods selected should fit the purposes.

Partnerships

Hopkins et al. (1994: p119) describe three forms of partnership between teachers, where classroom observation can be used for feedback, reflection and change.

Peer observation refers to the observation of one person's teaching by another. If this is done on an exchange basis it 'quickly breaks down barriers and encourages collaboration'. The observer can play differing roles, looking at the lesson in general or focusing on specific aspects of teaching. It is often helpful for them to look at the response of pupils, and to note incidents that the teacher might miss. Time must be set aside for feedback, and many teachers will find it helpful to have some training in methods of recording and analysing what they see. This approach is valuable, since teachers often learn best from other teachers. If a school is convinced of its worth, then the resources to support it must be found.

A set of questions that can be used for peer observation is:
- What did the pupils actually do?
- What were they learning?
- Was it worth it?
- What did the teacher do?

and for reflection afterwards:
- What have we learned?
- What do we intend to do now?

Clinical supervision is a rather daunting name given to a more formal process between teachers that incorporates a planning meeting, then some classroom observation, and is followed by a feedback meeting. The climate needs to be helping and trusting. The focus of observation is more specifically related to improvement, and it is suggested that it should be about reinforcing successful patterns rather than criticism. It resembles the fourth level of Tann and Griffiths' model in that it depends on the collection of data, not value judgements. The teachers together should make inferences from the data and test these out. Each cycle would be part of an ongoing process, with new focuses related to the last piece of planning. It is a shared process, and teachers can take it in turns to observe each other.

Coaching is more closely focused on support for a specific change. The teacher who is 'coach' works with the other teacher on a specific concern, and on identifying what the teacher needs to change. The role of coach is a suitable one for subject co-ordinators, and those with specific subject expertise, to take on if time can be found. It would be a useful approach to use in secondary schools to support teachers who find themselves deployed to teach subjects with which they are less familiar (for instance religious education, or personal and social education).

School Planning Sheet 7, shown on page 210, can be adapted and applied to provide a structure for identifying an observation focus, and some points for reflection, for any of the above partnerships.

Focusing classroom visits

Some classroom monitoring may be used regularly, by head-teachers and heads of department, to check up on routine activities, such as seeing that teachers are covering what they plan to do, checking homework diaries, and looking at the use of assessment and the appropriateness of tasks for different pupils. A whole-school theme, such as the use of assessment, raising expectations, the pace of lessons or the range of activities, can form the basis for classroom visits. The purposes and criteria should nonetheless be discussed between the observer and observed.

A school that is about to experience an external inspection, or one that has taken on the OFSTED criteria for teaching, may wish to focus observation round these questions from the *Framework*:

- Do teachers have a secure knowledge and understanding of the subjects or areas they teach?
- Do teachers set high expectations so as to challenge pupils and deepen their knowledge and understanding?
- Do teachers plan effectively?
- Do teachers employ methods and organisational strategies which match curricular objectives and the needs of all pupils?
- Do teachers manage well and achieve high standards of discipline?

- Do teachers use time and resources effectively?
- Do teachers assess pupils' work thoroughly and constructively and use assessments to inform teaching?
- Do teachers use homework effectively to reinforce and/or extend what is learnt in school?

Although there are only eight questions here, they are very basic questions that any teacher is likely to agree are at the heart of their teaching. It may be helpful to translate them out of OFSTED-speak into features that are recognisable in the particular classroom, and a means of doing that is suggested in School Planning Sheet 8 (shown on page 211).

Ensuring monitoring makes a difference

Underlying much school improvement theory is the assumption that if a school or a teacher understands their strengths and weaknesses, and has a commitment to improve and the skill and expertise to plan how to improve, then there will be effective action and positive change. An essential part of this process is the 'action plan', required at the level of the school after OFSTED inspection, and also seen as part of the response to the intervention of outside observation, analysis and feedback related to an individual teacher's work. The more formal the observation, and the more systematic the reflection, the more need there is for a written, shared plan of action. Informal replanning takes place at Tann and Griffiths' first three levels. Written action plans may be required in more formal monitoring procedures, and may also be useful within less formal, voluntary partnerships as a means of learning together by making reflections more precise.

Developing practice in a first school

The headteacher of a first school described the first years of introducing monitoring and peer partnerships in this way: 'It's taken about three years for me to establish a culture whereby staff really can understand why we monitor. We used to call it the m-word. I think we are about 75 per cent there now. People say things like 'we've got to check up on this to see that it is happening'.

The school uses peer partnerships in several ways. When the idea was first introduced teachers each chose a 'learning partner'; they selected a focus and observed each other's lessons, giving feedback and planning action which they reviewed again. The headteacher remembers that they first had to be clear about the difference between appraisal and the partnerships – it was important to explore and establish, for the whole staff, levels of trust, honesty, openness and confidentiality.

They used planning sheets to record what they planned to do together, what they found out as a result of observation and discussion, and what they decided to do next. The headteacher found a variety of ways to cover classes so that these pairings of teachers could occur. On the second cycle each teacher was required to work with a different learning partner, and this has now been repeated four times.

After learning partnerships were well established the school introduced peer observations of a different sort (with different partners) called 'checking partnerships'. In this sort of partnership there was an agreed whole-school focus and a teacher would ask a colleague for specific feedback about things she or he was endeavouring to change. Each of the two teachers chose three targets to meet, and these were checked on three times with the same partner.

During the course of the school year the school now provides time for staff to explore their own learning, as well as time for 'checking partners' with a focus on agreed school policy and practice.

Teachers reported that both sorts of partnerships had been useful: 'long term benefits for my classroom practice'; 'the benefits for me are sharing problems, pressures and workload'; 'the possibilities of change are stimulating – sometimes worrying, but challenging too'.

As well as the peer partnerships the school uses a system of 'school management monitoring' which arises from the identification of 'critical incidents'. Most recently this has led to a whole–school focus on improving the teaching of reading. A staff development day on this topic generated 14 different issues (which were used as evaluation features, as in the cycle described in Chapters 4 and 5). On the head-teacher's visit to a classroom both she and the teacher know that these are issues that she might be looking at. This arrangement has elements of formality and informality. The criteria are implicit but nevertheless shared, because of the joint planning which has identified this as an important area for improvement. The headteacher feeds back to individual teachers immediately (at break, at lunchtime, or after school) or makes time for a longer session if the observations need more discussion in depth. She summarises what she has seen in several visits (say five or six) at senior management team meetings (headteacher, deputy and key stage co-ordinators). The school will also report in a different way to governors on the reading initiative, and has commissioned an external consultant's report on literacy in the school.

Even with this variety of initiatives the headteacher acknowledges that what is most difficult is to evaluate whether what a teacher is doing makes a real difference to the progress of an individual child. The school is working on improving their methods to ensure that review partnerships really shift attitudes and make things change.

Successful improvement

For classroom observation strategies to result in actual improvement several conditions appear to be necessary:

- good diagnostic evaluation as a positive experience for the school;
- co-operative action planning;
- capacity to implement action plans;
- interest and involvement of parents;
- access to appropriate advice, support and training;
- identification of resources for development;
- setting targets to be achieved in specified time;
- effective monitoring of progress.

While valuing an element of formality in action planning and recording findings it is important not to lose sight of the value of serendipity. The heroes of the fairy tale *The Three Princes of Serendip* were always 'making discoveries, by accidents and sagacity, of things they were not in quest of', so serendipity is 'the faculty of making happy and unexpected discoveries by accident'. Not every important outcome can be envisaged and planned for.

It is important, also, to allow the teacher's own definition of successful change to emerge, and to be discussed, as this quotation from a teacher in an elementary school in the United States illustrates:

> I was using assertiveness discipline. My peer observer came in and just said 'Why is that important? What does it do?' I just had to explain what it did. I am making these kids work for rewards. Just talking about it I thought this is crazy. Why am I doing this? I didn't come to a conclusion. But later I kept thinking about it. That's right, they are only doing this for a reward. I've got to stop this. So I haven't done it since the conference. I don't have the control, but I'm using an approach I believe in. Next year I will start from the beginning with a more intrinsic approach.
>
> (Gitlin and Smyth, 1989)

Trust, creativity and confidence

Throughout this chapter the main concern has been with creating the conditions for teachers to feel secure enough to reflect and share their insights and feelings about their teaching. Good school management recognises the value of collaboration and collegiality in linking teacher development to school effectiveness. It is the responsibility of management to generate the right climate, as well as techniques, skills and commitment.

Tutors at the University of Cambridge Institute of Education describe the powerful nature of the experience of teachers who begin to think about, and change, their approach to teaching. They note that:

> Teachers have learned to live in a crowd, to some extent in control, but always aware of an audience – they can always feel other people's eyes on them, and are always conscious of the effect – or lack of it – of their words and deeds. Yet paradoxically teachers often experience a sense of isolation.
>
> (Drummond and McLaughlin, 1994: p 35)

With their students these tutors have found it necessary to acknowledge the emotional dimension of learning. Course members said: 'I was surprised to find I was the only one who couldn't cope, and some days you wondered why you were ever a teacher'; 'I was surprised that everyone felt as threatened as I did'; 'I was surprised to find that most teachers feel they have shortcomings'.

These teachers were working out of their normal school environment, and had chosen the course of study. These feelings of insecurity and self-doubt are also present for teachers engaged in development work with colleagues they see every day. Andy Hargreaves (1994) has some telling points to make about teachers and guilt. One teacher involved in a study of time spent on preparation said: 'You go home, you always have stuff that you think about. You think "I should be doing this"; you feel guilty sitting down half the time.' Managers attempting to generate practical strategies for collaboration cannot afford to ignore these emotions in their colleagues.

The Cambridge tutors list five principles that they see as important for their mature students on in-service courses. These principles have just as much relevance for those who wish to create in school a climate for shared reflection which is designed to lead to change in practice.

For consideration

Principles for teacher development

Does this climate exist in the school? How can it be developed?

Teachers need:

- a sense of purpose and determination;

the exercise of self-questioning has to seem intrinsically worthwhile;

- a sense of control;

there has to be a sense that what a teacher is doing at present is basically OK;

- a sense of support;

ways of challenging do not damage the teachers' commitment to what they are doing;

- a sense of self;

people learn to change effectively within a safe environment to explore;

- a sense of success;

within a supportive group teachers can talk about what they do well and about what they are learning to do better.

(adapted from Drummond and McLaughlin, 1994)

It is difficult to explore and change what you do as a teacher even in an off-site course. The uncertainties that emerge, and the need to take the emotional dimension of learning into account, are a little easier to discuss in a group where members do not have to maintain day-to-day working relationships. When groups and teams from a school staff work together the emotional dimension is there, but it is more deeply hidden in school and it may not feel safe to admit uncertainty and to explore. Curriculum leaders will need either to temper their expectations with realism, or to take some calculated risks, and see what changes. Successful change does not happen in a school situation without some disturbance, and some destabilisation of former apparently secure social relationships.

Susan Rosenholtz's findings from 78 elementary schools in Tennessee compensate for this concern by presenting vivid pictures of the contrast between schools that risk this disturbance and those that remain 'stuck':

We observed that without learning opportunities, task autonomy, and psychic rewards, teachers' sense of commitment seemed choked by a string of broken promises. Most lost their faith in their energies and values...it seemed a heavy burden to carry this weight of destructive scepticism. Conversely, in learning enriched settings, an abundant spirit of continuous improvement seemed to hover school-wide, and no one ever stopped learning to teach. Principals' frequent and useful evaluations seemed also a powerful mechanism for delivery on the promise of school improvement, as they also served as guides for future work.

(Rosenholtz, 1989)

There are more recent, and geographically closer, accounts of such environments. For instance, the 'success against the odds' of a primary school in Manchester is described (National Commission on Education,1996) as 'based on mutual trust. This trust allows people not only to feel safe, but to be challenged... Both staff and children feel safe to make, admit to, and learn from mistakes and to share worries and concerns.'

7 Building partnerships for success

Schools should select distinctive ways of improving from within. Effective schools choose a range of processes, involving a range of people, with the aim of knowing more about the school community in order to work better for the benefit of pupils.

This chapter looks at the partnerships that must be built in order to use school self-review as a means of improvement. Parents, governors and other members of the local community have a legitimate interest in the success of the school, and can be a source of support. External inspection, and a consequent public identification of weaknesses in some schools, is a source of stress, but has, ultimately, to be used in combination with the school's own procedures. The school can choose its external support, in the form of advice and training, from a range of LEA advisers, consultants and higher education institutions. 'Failing schools' may be special cases, needing particular support. The internal partnership, based on a shared commitment to creating a learning organisation, is one important force for change, and must be skilfully managed to focus on outcomes for pupils.

Partnership with the community

The school has a responsibility to the community as a whole, and endeavours to work through partnership with parents, whose concerns will be primarily for their own children. This sometimes presents dilemmas and tensions. Joan Sallis (1988) lists some fundamental questions about a public education service:

- how can we create and sustain enough public commitment to an adequately resourced system?
- how can we reconcile acceptable minimum standards in all schools with the demand for local variety and freedom, the need to foster creativity and the desire of parents for choice?
- how can we reconcile choice for parents with equal opportunity for children, given that the desire for choice arises from, feeds on and perpetuates inequality?

These questions, posed by a committed governor of schools, with long experience of the education system in the United Kingdom, are some of the most fundamental and challenging that face schools and the education service. She responds to her own questions by arguing that the partnership between teachers, parents and governors must be based on a sense of accountability which accepts a shared responsibility for success 'at the level of the child, the school and the service'.

One of the effects of well-managed school self-review should be to generate this sense of partnership in working for success at the school level. For parents this includes working with teachers for the success of their own child, but goes more widely than that, as they become involved in a review of what the school is aiming to do for all, and the action that follows. The self-interest of the individual and the forces of the market place are, on their own, insufficient to improve the network of provision in all our schools. To build up a sense of shared responsibility, parents, governors and other members of the local community should be involved in school review in several different ways.

Parental involvement in school review

Identifying targets and areas to evaluate

At a practical level the concerns of parents and the local community should be reflected in the targets the schools sets itself, and in choice of particular areas of the school's work for in-depth evaluation. The governing body, in that it represents parents and others in the local area, has a key role in setting and publicising the aims of the school, and the specific targets that it is hoping to achieve (Audit Commission, 1995). Local knowledge is important in setting realistic targets. Governors can also take account of other information, such as comparative information about other schools from performance tables, from contextual information provided for schools that are about to be inspected (a document called the Pre-inspection Context and School Indicator report, or PICSI), from Audit Commission reports and from the annual report of Her Majesty's Chief Inspector of Schools (HMCI).

The importance of taking a national view, and having ambitions for the success of all young people, is underlined in the annual report for 1993/4:

> The issue of whether enough is currently expected of children who live in areas characterised by high levels of social and economic disadvantage is particularly pressing. Such children should not be assumed to be intrinsically less intelligent than their more fortunate peers... We need sustained action, institutionally, locally and nationally if real and lasting improvements are to be achieved.
>
> (OFSTED, 1995a: p7)

In the following year's report the concern is still noted, but some success commended:

> Some schools serving extremely deprived areas achieve very good standards...teachers work together as a team, reviewing strengths and weaknesses, identifying priorities for action, and ensuring that in-service training is used to maximum effect. The culture is positive in the sense that the school believes in the possibility of success and takes responsibility for its failures.
>
> (OFSTED, 1996: p9)

Parents will have their own hopes, fears and expectations for the success of the schools serving their community. These should be taken into account in a school's aspirations, and evaluation. The approach to school self-evaluation of the team from the University of Strathclyde (MacBeath et al., 1996), described in Chapter 4, uses parents and governors not only in setting targets, but in the choice of areas to evaluate. The research team worked with schools where a collaborative approach to evaluation was seen as challenging, and where the involvement of the researchers was welcome. Sessions with groups of interested people (parents, governors, teaching and non-teaching staff and pupils) 'started early in the morning as parents arrived with their children and did not finish until late into the evening as the governors headed for home'.

Contributing evidence

Many evaluation exercises will seek parents' views either informally through discussion or, sometimes, through surveys and questionnaires. To keep in touch with what parents want a school should regularly survey parents, using a small number of criteria which allow comparisons and indicators of improvement to be made over time.

Analysing information

Some governors (and some parents) may be willing to become involved in analysing evidence gathered as part of an evaluation exercise, and in working with teachers on the best way to present information to other members of the community.

Reading and hearing reports

The statutory annual reports to parents are not always effective in involving people with the work of the whole-school, and in many areas annual parents' meetings are very poorly attended. These ways of communicating are, at present, required by law; but a school can be flexible, and find additional means of communicating with parents.

The Parent's Charter (DFE, 1994) sees the main aim of communicating with parents as for the parent to receive 'all the information you need to make decisions about your child's education', and 'the information you need when you are choosing your child's next school'. The school that is ambitious to achieve a partnership which ensures that the needs of the whole community are considered, by each individual involved, will want to devise informative ways of communicating the range and variety of the school's work.

Being involved in action

The Parent's Charter also recommends that parents 'get the best education for your child' by acting as active partners with the school and its teachers. It suggests to parents the importance of supporting the school's policy on homework and behaviour, and indicates that there are opportunities for parents to volunteer to share skills and interests with pupils and teachers.

The importance of the links between home and school are increasingly stressed in the policy documents of the political parties. Schools that have worked on home–school liaison for years, but find the initiatives increasingly difficult to fund, will find some irony in this policy support without further resources. In whatever way it can be resourced, however, it is important to build on the awareness of parents which can be generated by collaborative evaluation to involve them further in the action that affects their children.

External inspection, support and advice

OFSTED Inspection

In setting up new systems for self-review a school needs to find an appropriate balance between central direction and firm leadership, and fostering the creativity of individuals and departments to use the systems in ways that work for them. This calls for a balance of pressure and support. The introduction of regular school inspections, by OFSTED teams, with regular public reporting, is one (often painful) element of external pressure. Even schools that are developing their own self-review systems with some confidence may find it difficult to welcome external inspectors as partners in this process.

The inspection *Framework* emphasises that such a partnership is genuinely intended:

> The inspection process should help the school to raise educational standards. The governors and staff need

to be involved as far as possible in the inspection. Where possible, inspectors should discuss with the staff the context of work observed, its purpose, and reasons why work is undertaken in a particular way. It is good practice for inspectors to test hypotheses with staff before judgements are finalised. In that an inspection, of necessity, takes place over a short period of time, inspectors should consider the school's own priorities for development, evidence about the past attainments of pupils and any evidence from the school's own analysis of its provision and standards.

(OFSTED, 1995b: para 10)

The OFSTED official view is that inspection should give a school a firm platform for development and self-review. Moreover, to be of the greatest benefit, the inspection should be assimilated into the school's own mechanism for monitoring standards and improving quality.

The first cycle of OFSTED inspections has had a strong impact on schools' cultures and expectations about accountability.

An outside team conducting an external inspection brings to any school a freshness of vision, an awareness of what might be done differently. Are any of us that honest in our self-scrutiny?... I have no doubt that external inspection has helped to create a climate of accountability in which there is a new commitment, a greater urgency, in schools to deal with problems and raise standards.

(HMCI, writing in the Guardian of 6 February 1996)

Many schools have been impelled to improve their monitoring and review system as a result of questions asked by inspectors, particularly as questions are asked about progress on the action plan. The post-inspection action plans of the first schools to be inspected were criticised:

Whilst monitoring was undertaken in many schools, few schools had effective methods for evaluating the outcomes of their plans. They did not distinguish sufficiently well between monitoring – checking that they had done what they set out to do – and evaluation – judging its effectiveness... A lack of evaluation meant that most schools did not have adequate means of checking that their plans would result in demonstrably improved standards in the classroom. Governors and teachers would benefit from training in school evaluation with these outcomes in mind.

(OFSTED, 1995c: p 20)

For there to be genuine partnership between external evaluation and school self-review there needs to be a real integration of the concepts, based on consideration of the principles set out below:

- the conduct and focus of the external review is discussed and negotiated in the school;
- criteria used in external evaluation are disseminated and discussed and made meaningful to those to whom they apply;
- there is a protocol of behaviour, interpersonal relationships and professional respect which is understood and agreed;
- the school has faith in the competence and credibility of the review team;
- the review team contains a mixture of people, some of whom are familiar with the school and some of whom have no prior knowledge;
- review teams are accountable for the quality of their work;
- the process is seen by the key stakeholders as worthwhile and as supporting school and classroom development;
- responsibilities for evaluation are shared between external and internal sources as appropriate;
- the focus of the external review is primarily on the quality of the school's own approach to self-improvement and

on its capacity for change;

- the review team takes time to get to know the school and its community before embarking on an 'inspection'.

(MacBeath et al., 1996: p 90)

Advice and support

A school has complete control of its agenda for development, through its action plan or development plan. Except in the case of schools judged to be 'failing to give an acceptable standard of education', which are seen to need special treatment, decisions about external support and advice are firmly in the hands of the school and its governors. In practice many schools buy in to a contract guaranteeing so many days of support and training from local education authority (LEA) advisory teams.

These teams are more in demand than they ever were, but, in many areas of the country, there are fewer specialist advisers, and many of them have to spend some of their time on contracts to inspect schools. The new unitary authorities, set up under local government reorganisation in 1996 and 1997, have not the resources to employ a full range of subject specialist advisers. Institutes of higher education are extending their provision of in-service training, of modular, part-time, award-bearing courses at master's and doctorate level, and of conferences and consultancy activities. There are a number of private agencies, large and small, offering consultancy, advice and support.

Ideally, a school should have knowledge of, and access to, all these varieties of support. In practice the time it would take to become sufficiently well informed to act as a truly discriminating purchaser of services means that schools tend to rely on trusted 'critical friends', and word-of-mouth recommendations. OFSTED warns of a 'culture of dependency', yet the stress of external inspection has, in some instances, contributed to the uncertainty of those leading schools about the extent and nature of the support they need.

School Planning Sheet 9 (shown on page 212) sets out a framework for making decisions about where support is most needed, for costing it, and for beginning to identify the most appropriate provider. Although such provision will take place as a partnership, it is important for a school to recognise the commercial dimension, to make sure that it gets value for money, and to do this through a very professional process of deciding what is really needed, and making a contract on that basis with the provider.

The TTA and OFSTED publish their Corporate Plans annually. The plans set out the targets for these agencies, in terms of the ways that their work can give support to the action for school improvement in individual institutions. The LEA and its advisory services will have similar Strategic Plans. The school should form its own plans to use support in the light of the information from these documents, as well as from publicity material and advertisements in the educational press.

The special case of failing schools

There is a different attitude to the 'failing' or 'struggling' school, well illustrated by the comments of Michael Barber (1995). He said that schools which are failing or struggling 'infringe the rights' of numbers of young people, and claimed that one distinction between 'struggling' and 'failing' schools and others is the lack of a capacity to improve from within. National strategies should be based on increasing this capacity within all schools, but initially the 'failing' group of schools need help to develop this ability to improve. 'External intervention in a school's affairs should be in inverse proportion to its success.'

The failing school is seen to be a very special case, and to need a particular sort of partnership with outsiders to help it to change. It is argued that a failing school does not merely lack the characteristics of effective schools, but has distinctly different characteristics, which reinforce the sense of failure. Failing schools seem to have cultures where collaboration has broken down, where there is conflict between staff and a reluctance to stand out and express a point of view because of a fear of failure or the consequences of failure. They are likely to need help in the areas of their formal organisation, their culture and expectations, and in the areas of relationships. The most vulnerable schools will often find it hard to take on self-evaluation as a force to improve things. Self-review may not get to the heart of long-standing problems. Some guidance will be needed, as will special approaches to action and to review.

Government Grants for Education Support and Training (GEST) set aside funding for LEAs and schools to use in this predicament. Initially schools in difficulties are advised to use their money to purchase external expertise in the action planning process that follows inspection. The identification of a school as 'failing' (the legal term is 'in need of special measures') or in the category of 'schools with serious weaknesses', guarantees that there will be monitoring visits on a regular basis by Her Majesty's Inspectors (HMI) from OFSTED. The principle of planning, action, monitoring and review is still applied, but outside pressure and support is provided frequently, and is seen as essential. Fundamentally, however, the role of any intervention should be to generate within a school the capacity for 'sustainable self-renewal'.

David Reynolds (1996) speculates that change in ineffective schools may best be attempted by bringing in the outside knowledge and confidence that a school needs in the form of a school insider, rather than in the form of a 'threatening' outsider. He recognises that new ideas will be more effective if they are attached to a person, rather than being expected to take root through a process of 'cultural diffusion'.

Concern about the possibility and pace of change underlies all these speculations about the fate of failing schools. There is a growing number of success stories, however. In one primary school, designated as failing, a new headteacher was seconded to take the lead in the term after the adverse inspection report. Before accepting the invitation to take up the secondment he assessed the situation for himself. He asked for specific promises from the LEA about the speed with which support of various kinds would be made available to the school. He fits David Reynolds's description of the school insider motivating change; he became a real insider by applying for, and being appointed, to the headship shortly after his secondment. He worked for a year before getting a report from the OFSTED team that the school was 'no longer in need of special measures'.

His recipe for success with a 'failing' school includes these ingredients:

- a high level of support from LEA, especially from advisers, finance and personnel officers;
- a timetable for action planning;
- clarity about the leadership role of the headteacher – once something is policy it is non-negotiable, everyone complies;
- openness with staff;
- expectation of commitment – hard work, low absence, people should be prepared to be honest;
- orderly working environment;
- involvement of local people, dealing with the effect on the community, and on parents, of the public announcement of failure;
- involvement of governors at all stages;
- ownership of success.

In this climate he used external monitoring and evaluation (from the LEA and from OFSTED) to create a new, positive ethos of success which was publicly celebrated. The particular circumstances of the school, and the fact that its status placed it in the public eye, meant that such reporting had to be honest and frank. Within the school, issues of weakness and lack of competence could not be hidden or ignored.

The learning organisation

The most creative sort of partnership for any school is the internal one, where the school believes itself to be a 'learning organisation'. The description of the experience of the school in the previous section shows that this sense of learning together can be fostered, even under unlikely and difficult circumstances. It also illustrates that the concept of a learning organisation is not a 'soft option' for any school.

These are characteristics of a school which is a learning organisation:

- the school presents learning as something which is for the adults working there as well as for pupils;
- the school provides training and development for all its staff, including school-based staff development.

Such an institution will seek to find ways of using school self-review, as described in this book, to enhance the capacity of the individuals who work there. It will recognise that individuals come to accept and participate in change in ways that change them personally, and that may be threatening and may be exciting. Change may mean new knowledge, new skills and new perceptions of pupils and colleagues. The organisation will have values that determine the outcomes it sees as important to target and monitor; there need to be ways of finding out if all those who work there subscribe to the values, and ways of debating them to reinforce a common understanding.

Plans for in-service training (continuous professional development) will take account of the need for individuals to change, and to contribute creatively to changes in their own teaching, and in that of others. The TTA sees it as a priority 'to ensure that investment in in-service training and development should result in direct improvements in the classroom in order to raise standards of pupils' performance'. The agency argues that schools need to

- use their resources, largely GEST and the five school closure days, as part of a planned, co-ordinated approach;
- follow up professional development activities to see what impact they have;
- target professional development activities to identified needs;
- co-ordinate on-the-job development opportunities;
- expect teachers to set their own targets for improvement.

The TTA recognises the importance of development that takes place on the school site, and that is related to school targets and to school plans. International work on school improvement suggests that the learning organisation will have features such as those listed below:

- a high degree of school and classroom based staff development;
- a range of teaching styles and models;
- reflection by teachers on the way they teach;
- work in partnership with colleagues to focus on the improvement of teaching;
- involvement of pupils in teaching and learning process;
- ways of sustaining innovation through clear leadership roles;
- effective use of external support and outside consultants.

(Hopkins et al., 1994)

In such an organisation the notion of accountability would be less of a threat and more of an entitlement. Models of improvement that stress the need for an organisation to become a 'learning organisation' rely on the self motivation of individuals, and on a belief that all who participate have a legitimate interest in quality and progress. The accountability process is then democratic and egalitarian, in the sense that it requires all participants to see themselves as equally accountable to one another for their particular contributions to the educational process. The organisation's approach to innovation and improvement assumes that the situation of staff and the quality of school life are powerful influences on, and matter as much as, the learning experiences of pupils. The school demonstrates a belief that people are capable of creative action if conditions are made more favourable. It recognises that changing attitudes and relationships is as important as gaining new skills.

There may seem to be a complete polarisation between the empowerment model described above and the rational model that has underpinned much of the central advice that teachers in England have received about school self-review. The apparent 'opposites' are set out in Figure 12 below.

Figure 12 **Approaches to self-review**

Creativity and development?	**Rationality and accountability?**
Collaboration and involvement	Leadership
Democracy	Hierarchy
Spontaneity	Planning to meet targets
Empowerment	Monitoring
Creativity and commitment	Sustaining progress
Benefits for the individual	Rigorous evaluation
Celebrating successes	Remedying weaknesses

To view these concepts as in opposition is unfortunate and unnecessary. In practice the tensions have to be resolved in the school. How can the concepts be made to work together? Leadership should foster collaboration and inspire involvement, the clarity of roles in a hierarchy should determine responsibilities, and democracy and spontaneity be used to generate imaginative and acceptable courses of action. Planning gives a reality to the directions chosen and can empower people, monitoring can be used to sustain progress, evaluation credits the experience and perceptions of individuals with some validity, and success is not ignored although reflection may lead to self criticism. If individual commitment is valued, creative ideas fostered, and if the whole operation leads to benefits that are experienced as meaningful, then the blending process is complete.

Whatever the ways that are used to create a learning organisation, school leaders need to provide clarity, firmness and reminders of expectations. Flexibility and sensitivity can enable teachers to develop for themselves, but the expectations and requirements of heads of department, and of headteachers, need to be made both clear and manageable, or the defensive response will be to claim confusion and overload. Ultimately measures of success have to be not only school-specific, but specific and relevant to each teacher and pupil. Monitoring and support at school level are the most salient requirements in sustaining improvement, and these need to encourage, as well as require, the co-operation of teachers in changes intended to raise standards. New practices will be sustained if they are seen to be of direct benefit, not only to pupils, but to teachers in their working lives.

Appendix 1:
School profile based on OFSTED criteria

What are the strengths and weaknesses of the school?

Standards and progress

1 How does the attainment of pupils at the end of key stages compare with national standards?

2 Do all pupils, including those with special educational needs, make good progress in their learning?

3 Is the progress made by members of minority groups comparable with that of others in the school?

Pupils' attitudes

4 Do pupils show independence and initiative?

5 Do they work collaboratively when required, and can

they take responsibility for personal study?

6 Do they behave courteously and show a respect for property?

7 Do they form good relationships and show respect for other people's feelings?

8   Are attendance and punctuality satisfactory?

Teaching

9   Do teachers have good knowledge of the subjects they teach?

10   Do they have high expectations and challenge the pupils to deepen their knowledge and understanding?

11   Do they plan effectively, to cover the material and to use time and resources effectively?

12   Do they employ methods which match the needs of all pupils?

13   Do they manage class discipline well?

14   Do they assess pupils' work thoroughly and use assessments to plan teaching?

15   Is homework used effectively?

16 Do the qualifications and experience of teachers and other classroom staff meet the demands of the curriculum?

Curriculum

17 Does what is taught prepare pupils for the next stage of education?

18 Is there equality of access and opportunity for pupils to learn and to make progress?

19 Does the curriculum meet the requirements of all pupils on the school's Code of Practice Special Educational Needs register?

20 Is there continuity and progression in curriculum planning?

21 Is there extra-curricular provision, including sport, to enrich what is provided ?

22 In secondary schools is there good careers guidance?

Spiritual, social, cultural and moral development of pupils

23 Does the school enable pupils to reflect on their experiences in a way which develops their self-knowledge and spiritual awareness?

24 Does the school teach principles which separate right from wrong?

25 Does the school encourage pupils to participate fully in the school community, and to understand the meaning of citizenship?

26 Does the school teach pupils to appreciate a range of cultural traditions?

Parents and community

27 Do parents have sound information about their children's progress and feel able to contribute to pupils' learning?

28 Does the school fully use its links with the community?

Leadership and management

29 Are there clear aims and a clear educational direction for the school?

30 Does the school monitor the academic progress, personal development, behaviour and attendance of pupils?

31 Are teaching and curriculum development monitored, evaluated and supported, and do arrangements for the professional development of staff contribute to their effective-ness?

32 Does the school choose its own priorities and targets and plan and take the necessary action to achieve them?

33 Does the school promote discipline and good behaviour and endeavour to eliminate harassment and bullying?

34 Does the school successfully promote the health, safety and general well-being of its pupils?

35 Are educational developments supported through careful financial planning, and efficient financial control?

36 Does the school provide value for money?

Appendix 2:
Subject profile based on OFSTED criteria

What are the strengths and weaknesses in the subject?

1 How does the attainment of the pupils compare with attainment in the subject nationally?

2 Is there improvement in overall attainment over time?

3 Do pupils make good progress in the subject?

4 Do pupils have good attitudes to learning in the subject?

5 Is there significant variation in attainment or progress of boys and girls?

6 Is there significant variation in attainment or progress of different ethnic groups?

7 Is the National Curriculum covered, if appropriate?

8 Do teachers have a good knowledge and understanding of the subject?

9 Do they have high expectations of pupils' achievement?

10 Do they plan effectively, to cover the material and to use time and resources effectively?

11 Do they employ methods which match the needs of all pupils?

12 Do they manage class discipline well?

13 Is formative assessment used to plan teaching?

14 Is homework used effectively?

15 Do the qualifications and experience of teachers and other classroom staff meet the demands of the curriculum?

16 Is the curriculum well planned for continuity and progression of learning?

17 Are there consistently applied systems for assessing pupils' attainment?

18 Are teaching and curriculum development monitored, evaluated and supported?

19 Does the department choose its priorities and targets, and plan and take action to achieve them?

20   Are there effective arrangements for the induction, appraisal and professional development of staff?

21   Does the accommodation allow the subject to be taught effectively?

22   Are learning resources adequate for the subject and range of pupils needs?

References

AUDIT COMMISSION (1995) *Lessons in Teamwork: How School Governing Bodies Can Become More Effective*. London, HMSO.

BARBER M (1995) Shedding Light on the Dark Side of the Moon (Greenwich Lecture) *Times Educational Supplement* 12 May 1995.

BEMAS Conference (1995) *Leaders and Leadership in Schools and Colleges*. (Publication edited by Peter Ribbins, forthcoming. London, Cassell.)

BOYD B, MACBEATH J and RAND J (1995) Towards a Framework for Self Evaluation in *Managing Schools Today* Vol 5 no 2 pp 21–24.

CALDWELL B and SPINKS J (1988) *The Self-Managing School*. London, Falmer.

COOPERS & LYBRAND (1988) *Local Management of Schools*. London, HMSO.

DES (1989) *Planning for School Development*. London, HMSO.

DFE (1994) *Our Children's Education: The Updated Parent's Charter*. London, HMSO.

DFE (1995a) *Governing Bodies and Effective Schools*. London, Department for Education.

DFE (1995b) *Value Added in Education*. London, Department for Education.

DFE (1995c) *GCSE to GCSE A/AS Value Added*. London, Department for Education.

DFEE (1996) *Setting Targets to Raise Standards: A Survey of Good Practice*. London, Department for Education and Employment.

DRUMMOND M J and McLAUGHLIN C (1994) 'Teaching and Learning – The Fourth Dimension' in *Developing Teachers, Developing Schools*, H Bradley, C Conner and G Southworth (eds) London, Fulton.

GITLIN A and SMYTH J (1989) *Teacher Evaluation: Educative Alternatives*. Lewes, Falmer.

GRIFFITHS M and TANN S (1992) Using Reflective Practice to Link Personal and Public Theories in *Journal of Education for Teaching*, Vol 18, no 1 (pp 69-84).

HARGREAVES A(1994) *Changing Teachers, Changing Times*. London, Cassell.

HARGREAVES D (1994) *The Mosaic of Learning*. London, Demos.

HARGREAVES D (1995) Self Managing Schools and Development Planning in *School Organisation* Vol 15, no 3, p226.

HARGREAVES D and HOPKINS D (1991) *The Empowered School*. London, Cassell.

HOPKINS D, AINSCOW M and WEST M (1994) *School Improvement in an Era of Change*. London, Cassell.

LABOUR PARTY (1995) *Excellence for Everyone*. London, Labour Party.

LOUDEN W (1991) *Understanding Teaching*. London, Cassell.

MACBEATH J, BOYD B, RAND J and BELL S (1996) *Schools Speak for Themselves*. London, NUT.

NATIONAL COMMISSION ON EDUCATION (1996) *Success Against the Odds*. London, Routledge.

OFSTED (1994) *Improving Schools*. London, HMSO.

OFSTED (1995a) *Annual Report of Her Majesty's Chief Inspector of Schools*, Part 1: Standards and Quality in Education 1993/4. London, HMSO.

OFSTED (1995b) *The OFSTED Handbook for the Inspection of Schools*. London, HMSO.

OFSTED (1995c) *Planning Improvement (Schools' Post-inspection Action Plans)*. London, HMSO.

OFSTED (1995d) *Teaching Quality: The Primary Debate*. London, OFSTED.

OFSTED (1996) *Annual Report of Her Majesty's Chief Inspector of Schools*, Part 1: Standards and Quality in Education 1994/5. London, HMSO.

REYNOLDS D (1996) 'Turning round the ineffective school: some evidence and some speculations' in *Merging Traditions*, J Gray, D Reynolds, C Fitzgibbon and D Jesson (eds) London, Cassell.

ROSENHOLTZ, S (1989) *Teachers' Workplace: the social organisation of schools*. New York, Teachers' College Press.

SALLIS J (1988) *Schools, Parents and Governors: A New Approach to Accountability*. London, Routledge.

TEACHER TRAINING AGENCY (1995) *Initial Advice to the Secretary of State on the Continuing Professional Development of Teachers*. London, TTA.

WRAGG E C (1994) *An Introduction to Classroom Observation*. London, Routledge.

Sources of government publications

OFSTED Publications Centre, PO Box 6927, London E3 3NZ. Telephone: 0171-510 0180

HMSO Publications Centre, PO Box 276, London SW8 5DT. Telephone: 0171-873 9090

DFEE Publications Centre, PO Box 6927, London E3 3NZ. Telephone: 0171-510 0150   EMail: info@dfee.gov.uk

DFEE Public Enquiry Unit, Room LG.01, DFEE, Sanctuary Buildings, Great Smith Street, London SW1P 3BT. Telephone: 0171-925 5555   EMail: info@dfee.gov.uk

School planning sheets

The school planning sheets on the following pages are shown as illustrations, partially completed. They can be adapted for use in any school, as appropriate.

School planning sheet 1
Governors' overview of monitoring and evaluation

Areas of school life	*Curriculum*	*Assessment*	*Pupils' behaviour*	*Pupils' attitudes to learning*
Targets to be monitored	*Average points score at GCSE*		*Reduction in short-term exclusions*	
Features to be examined for quality		*Use of assessment to inform planning*		*Independent learning*
Evidence to be collected		*Departmental practice*		*Pupils' use of planners*
Reporting date	*Sept 1997*	*June 1998*	*March 1998*	*April 1998*
Level of planning (e.g. governors, senior management, head of department)	*HOD, SMT then governors*	*HOD meeting*	*Heads of year. Governors*	*All staff SMT*

Support for pupils with special educational needs	Links with parents	Leadership and communication	Teachers' professional development	Resources for learning
	Number applying for Y7 admission			
	Level of satisfaction with information received			
	May 1998			
	Deputy, then governors			

School planning sheet 2
Setting objectives and monitoring action

School objective
Improve reading standards in Years 5 and 6

Strategy and associated tasks
Improve methods of reading assessment.
Devise a structured programme for all readers.
Develop a record system for reading at Key Stage 2.
Increase the amount of time devoted to reading.
Increase the number of appropriate books.

Headings for reporting
1 *Assessment: method and frequency for each pupil.*
2 *Standards achieved and time spent on reading.*
3 *Review of resources and identification of needs.*
4 *Progress on development of structured programme.*
5 *Introduction and use of new pupil record system.*

Reporting schedule

When?	To whom?	Which indicators?
October	*All Y5 and Y6 teachers*	*1 and 2*
December	*Deputy headteacher*	*3 and 4*
December	*Headteacher*	*2 and 3*
January	*All Y5 and Y6 teachers*	*5*
February	*Governors*	*2 and 3*
May	*Headteacher*	*4*
July	*Deputy headteacher*	*1, 4 and 5*

School planning sheet 3
Choosing features for evaluation: (A) Future images

School focus

The independent learning of pupils

The future

My class would each know the work I expected of them in a week, and would keep a record of what they've done.
They get their own equipment.
They are good at listening and ask questions that help them to learn better.

Key features

- *Pupils' own records of work done.*
- *An efficient working atmosphere.*
- *Pupils' improvement in listening skills.*

School planning sheet 4
Choosing features for evaluation: (B) Summarising

School focus

The independent learning of pupils

The future

Pupils know what they are expected to do in each half term.

They know what skills they have to develop, and are aware of the knowledge they have gained.

They are confident in their application of this knowledge.

They recognise their successes.

They can see where they have to improve.

They can discuss what they have to do next with teachers, with their friends, and with their parents.

They ask for advice from their teachers.

They know what resources are available, both in the school and outside, and they use them in classwork and in homework.

They know what their homework is for, and how it helps their learning.

They understand the objective of each task, lesson or week's work.

They keep some sort of record of what they have done.

In lessons they question the teacher, and each other.

They can suggest new sources of information and lines of enquiry.

They listen to others, and put forward their own views.

They enjoy the challenge of learning that the school presents.

Features to be addressed in reports

1 *Pupils' awareness of achievements and targets.*
2 *Teachers' planning of each half term's work.*
3 *Opportunities for pupils, teachers and parents to discuss progress made.*
4 *Availability and use of resources.*
5 *Pupils' listening and speaking skills.*

School planning sheet 5
Choosing features for evaluation: (C) Generating a list

What do we want to achieve?

An environment that supports learning

What would we see?	**What would we hear?**
Children working on task	*Talk between teachers and children*
Bright clean classrooms	*Respect for one another*
Stimulating thought-provoking displays	*Parents praising the teachers' understanding of their children's needs*

School planning sheet 6P
Primary timetable for evaluation and action

Dates	1996 July	1996 Oct	1996 Dec	1997 Feb
Focus	Teaching quality		Parental involvement in reading	
Identifying features	All staff		Key stage teams	
Collection of evidence		In key stage teams	In key stage teams	
Analysis and interpretation				By head and deputy
Reporting				
Action planning				

1997 Apr	1997 Jun	1997 Oct	1997 Dec	1998 Feb	1998 Apr
		Use of IT resources			
		By IT coordinator			
Measuring reading standards and parental views			Survey by teachers involving pupils		
	By head and coordinator for EN			By head and IT coordinator	
To whole staff	To whole staff	To parents and governors			To staff and governors
	Rolling programme by subject coordinators		Staff recommend-ations to governors	To governors for resource decisions	

School planning sheet 6S
Secondary timetable for evaluation and action

Dates	1996 July	1996 Oct	1996 Dec	1997 Feb
Focus	Teaching quality		Pupils' behaviour	
Identifying features	All staff		Pastoral teams	
Collection of evidence		By department heads with department		By staff survey
Analysis and interpretation				By HOD group
Reporting				
Action planning				

1997 Apr	1997 Jun	1997 Oct	1997 Dec	1998 Feb	1998 Apr
	Working environment				
	Staff sub-group				
		By pupil survey			
	By pastoral teams			By senior management	
To deputy headteacher	To whole staff	To governors, with action plans	To governors		To governors
	In departments	In working groups			By governors

School planning sheet 7
Choosing features for classroom observation

What I do now

I try to give every pupil a chance to talk in French, and to listen to someone else. I want them to practise some new grammatical construction in writing, and I want them to learn something about France.

I do a lot of talking and questioning, and I set some paired and some individual activities.

What I think is important

I want them to enjoy learning French.
I want them to be technically accurate.
I want none of the pupils to be wasting time.

What I want to know more about

I think other people might say the room is noisy – what do you think of my control of the class?
I'm not sure I'm using the best course-book – what do the pupils get out of it? Are they on task when they are doing the paired work?
How can I give individual feedback about the writing and get everything else done?

Key features to look at

1 *Discipline and noise level.*

2 *Time management.*

3 *What are pupils doing?*

4 *Appropriateness of material.*

School planning sheet 8
Using OFSTED criteria for evaluating teaching

Criterion

Do teachers set high expectations so as to challenge pupils and deepen their knowledge and understanding?

Translation

Does each pupil get something out of the lesson, or are some of them just coasting along?
Do the activities interest and challenge them?
What have they learned?

What I do now

I do a recap at the beginning of the lesson and ask questions to find out how much they remember.
When I set the work I tell them what I expect them to learn.
I have some extension work for those that finish early.
I ask questions at the end of the lesson to sum up.

How you would know if I was successful

All the pupils would be busy.
They could discuss what they were doing and tell you what they had learned, showing some understanding.
My class questioning would make it clear what they had grasped and what is not yet understood.

I would like feedback about

Appropriateness of tasks.
How much they understand of the lesson objectives.
Whether I involve all the pupils in question and response.

School planning sheet 9
Selecting external advice and support

	Whole school	**Department or team**	**Individual**
Advice	*From adviser on methods for evaluating IT provision*		
Evaluation and feedback		*Review of work in science by LEA inspector: feedback to whole school*	
Courses out of school			*20 day maths course, art and design course, SEN course*
In school develop-ment	*INSET day on reading with planned follow-up*	*KSI team paired evaluations with involvement of consultant as facilitator*	
Higher degrees			*Deputy headteacher working with HE supervisor on M Ed dissertation on parental involvement*
Action research		*Nursery nurse and nursery teacher study of use of early years assessment*	

Index

∙ ∙